LAWS AND LEGISLATION

RULES AND RULEMAKING IN THE PATIENT PROTECTION AND AFFORDABLE CARE ACT

Laws and Legislation

Additional books in this series can be found on Nova's website under the Series tab.

Additional E-books in this series can be found on Nova's website under the E-book tab.

Health Care Issues, Costs and Access

Additional books in this series can be found on Nova's website under the Series tab.

Additional E-books in this series can be found on Nova's website under the E-book tab.

LAWS AND LEGISLATION

RULES AND RULEMAKING IN THE PATIENT PROTECTION AND AFFORDABLE CARE ACT

RAPHAEL KIPP
AND
VINCE CAPUTO
EDITORS

Nova Science Publishers, Inc.
New York

For permission to use material from this book please contact us:
Telephone 631-231-7269; Fax 631-231-8175
Web Site: http://www.novapublishers.com

Additional color graphics may be available in the e-book version of this book.

Library of Congress Cataloging-in-Publication Data

Rules and rulemaking in the Patient Protection and Affordable Care Act / editors, Raphael Kipp and Vince Caputo.
p. cm.
Includes index.
ISBN 978-1-61942-194-3 (soft cover)
1. United States. Patient Protection and Affordable Care Act. 2. Medical care--Law and legislation--United States. 3. Health insurance--Law and legislation--United States . 4. National health insurance--Law and legislation--United States. 5. Health care reform--United States. I. Kipp, Raphael. II. Caputo, Vince.
KF3605.A328201A2 2011a
344.7302'2--dc23
2011045790

Published by Nova Science Publishers, Inc. † New York

CONTENTS

Preface		**vii**
Chapter 1	Rulemaking Requirements and Authorities in the Patient Protection and Affordable Care Act (PPACA) *Curtis W. Copeland*	**1**
Chapter 2	Upcoming Rules Pursuant to the Patient Protection and Affordable Care Act: Spring 2011 Unified Agenda *Maeve P. Carey and Curtis W. Copeland*	**33**
Chapter 3	Initial Final Rules Implementing the Patient Protection and Affordable Care Act *Curtis W. Copeland*	**77**
Index		**103**

PREFACE

Federal regulations generally start with an act of Congress, and are the means by which statutes are implemented and many specific requirements are established. The Patient Protection and Affordable Care Act is a particularly noteworthy example of congressional delegation of rulemaking authority to federal agencies. This book identifies more than 40 provisions in PPACA that require, permit, or contemplate rulemaking by federal agencies to implement the legislation.

Chapter 1- Federal regulations generally start with an act of Congress, and are the means by which statutes are implemented and many specific requirements are established. The Patient Protection and Affordable Care Act (PPACA, P.L. 111-148, March 23, 2010) is a particularly noteworthy example of congressional delegation of rulemaking authority to federal agencies. This report identifies more than 40 provisions in PPACA (as amended by the Health Care and Education Reconciliation Act of 2010, P.L. 111-152, March 30, 2010) that require, permit, or contemplate rulemaking by federal agencies to implement the legislation.

Chapter 2- Congress delegates rulemaking authority to agencies for a variety of reasons and in a variety of ways. The Patient Protection and Affordable Care Act (PPACA; P.L. 111-148) is a particularly noteworthy example of congressional delegation of rulemaking authority to federal agencies. A previous CRS report identified more than 40 provisions in PPACA that require or permit the issuance of rules to implement the legislation.

One way for Congress to identify upcoming PPACA rules is by reviewing the Unified Agenda of Federal Regulatory and Deregulatory Actions, which is published twice each year (spring and fall) by the Regulatory Information Service Center (RISC), a component of the U.S. General Services

Administration, for the Office of Management and Budget's (OMB) Office of Information and Regulatory Affairs (OIRA). The Unified Agenda lists upcoming activities, by agency, in five separate categories or stages of the rulemaking process: the prerule stage, the proposed rule stage, the final rule stage, long-term actions, and completed actions. All entries in the Unified Agenda have uniform data elements, including the department and agency issuing the rule, the title of the rule, its Regulation Identifier Number (RIN), an abstract describing the nature of action being taken, and a timetable showing the dates of past actions and a projected date for the next regulatory action. Each entry also contains an element indicating the priority of the regulation (e.g., whether it is considered "economically significant" under Executive Order 12866, or whether it is considered a "major" rule under the Congressional Review Act).

Chapter 3- More than 40 provisions in the Patient Protection and Affordable Care Act (PPACA, P.L. 111-148, March 23, 2010, as amended) specifically require or permit federal agencies to issue regulations to implement the act's requirements. This report describes the final rules implementing PPACA that had been published in the *Federal Register* during the first 81/2 months of implementation.

As of December 7, 2010, at least 18 final rules had been issued implementing certain provisions in PPACA. An Appendix to this report lists these 18 final rules, including a summary of their requirements and their effective dates. PPACA specifically required that some of the rules be published. Other rules cited particular sections of PPACA as the statutory authority, but those sections did not specifically require the agencies to accomplish the underlying policy objectives through the rulemaking process. Most of the final rules were issued without a prior notice of proposed rulemaking, with the agencies often invoking the "good cause" exception in the Administrative Procedure Act (APA, 5 U.S.C. §551 *et seq.)* for not allowing the public to comment before the final rules were issued. In several of the rules, the issuing agencies also stated that Congress had specifically authorized the issuance of final rules without first issuing a proposed rule. Most of the final rules permitted post-promulgation public comments, with the comment periods ending on or after the dates that the rules took effect. Most of the rules were considered "economically significant" (i.e., with an annual impact on the economy of at least $100 million), so the agencies provided estimates of their costs, benefits, and transfers.

In: Rules and Rulemaking in the Patient... ISBN: 978-1-61942-194-3
Editors: Raphael Kipp and Vince Caputo © 2012 Nova Science Publishers, Inc

Chapter 1

RULEMAKING REQUIREMENTS AND AUTHORITIES IN THE PATIENT PROTECTION AND AFFORDABLE CARE ACT (PPACA)*

Curtis W. Copeland

SUMMARY

Federal regulations generally start with an act of Congress, and are the means by which statutes are implemented and many specific requirements are established. The Patient Protection and Affordable Care Act (PPACA, P.L. 111-148, March 23, 2010) is a particularly noteworthy example of congressional delegation of rulemaking authority to federal agencies. This report identifies more than 40 provisions in PPACA (as amended by the Health Care and Education Reconciliation Act of 2010, P.L. 111-152, March 30, 2010) that require, permit, or contemplate rulemaking by federal agencies to implement the legislation.

Where new regulations are required in PPACA, this report also describes provisions in the act that prescribe the substance of certain regulations, procedural requirements regarding the development of those

* This is an edited, reformatted and augmented version of a Congressional Research Service publication, CRS Report for Congress R41180, from www.crs.gov, dated February 18, 2011.

rules, and provisions that establish regulatory deadlines. Where PPACA permits, but does not require, certain regulations, the amount of discretion provided to the agencies appears to vary, as well as the implications of that discretion. In some cases, the agencies appear able to decide whether to take any action, and if so, whether that action takes the form of a regulation or some other method of policy implementation (e.g., adjudication, policy statements, guidance, or memoranda). Other sections in PPACA do not specifically require or permit the development of regulations, instead referring to regulations "issued by the Secretary" or "promulgated by the Secretary." If these sections refer to existing rules, then new regulations may not be needed.

The report indicates that PPACA gives federal agencies substantial responsibility and authority to "fill in the details" of the legislation through subsequent regulations. Although some regulations were required in 2010, it seems likely that other regulations will be issued for years, or even decades to come. Also, although Congress delegates rulemaking authority for a variety of reasons, the manner in which Congress does so can determine who makes those decisions, and in what manner. When Congress requires that a regulation be issued or made effective by a particular date, that it contain certain substantive elements, and that the rule be developed following certain procedures, then the delegation of legislative rulemaking authority is somewhat limited and Congress retains a measure of control over the subsequent policymaking process. On the other hand, Congress grants substantial discretion to the regulatory agencies when it gives the heads of those agencies broad authority to "prescribe such regulations as may be necessary." Even more discretion may be given to the agencies when Congress permits agencies to decide certain threshold issues. While the regulations are being developed, or after they are issued, Congress and individual Members have various oversight options, including oversight hearings, meeting with agency officials and filing comments, the Congressional Review Act, and restrictions on agency appropriations.

INTRODUCTION

Federal regulations generally start with an act of Congress and are the means by which statutes are implemented and specific requirements are established. In *Building a Legislative-Centered Public Administration*, David H. Rosenbloom succinctly described why regulations are important, why Congress delegates rulemaking authority to federal agencies, and congressional responsibilities when such delegations are made:

> Rulemaking and lawmaking are functional equivalents. Legislative (substantive) rules made by agencies have the force of law. When agencies make such rules, in effect they legislate. Congress can delegate its legislative authority to the agencies at its discretion for a wide variety of reasons: to alleviate its workload; to avoid a particularly nettlesome political issue; to focus highly specialized administrative expertise on a particular problem; for convenience; or simply because the agencies do not face the constraints of a legislature that is reconstituted every two years.... The agencies perform legislative functions for Congress at its discretion, pursuant to delegations of its authority. The Constitution's grant of legislative power to Congress encompasses a responsibility to ensure that delegated authority is exercised according to appropriate procedures.[1]

Patient Protection and Affordable Care Act

The Patient Protection and Affordable Care Act (PPACA, P.L. 111-148, March 23, 2010) is a particularly noteworthy example of congressional delegation of rulemaking authority to federal agencies.[2] PPACA contains numerous provisions stating that federal agencies "shall promulgate regulations," or "shall, by regulation" take certain actions to implement the legislation. In an article entitled "The War Isn't Over" that was posted on the *New England Journal of Medicine's* Health Care Reform Center shortly after PPACA was signed into law, Henry J. Aaron and Robert D. Reischauer said the following:

> Making the legislation a success requires not only that it survive but also that it be effectively implemented. Although the bill runs to more than 2000 pages, much remains to be decided. The legislation tasks federal or state officials with writing regulations, making appointments, and giving precise meaning to many terms. Many of these actions will provoke controversy.... Far from having ended, the war to make health care reform an enduring success has just begun. Winning that war will require administrative determination and imagination and as much political resolve as was needed to pass the legislation.[3]

An article in *CQ Weekly* made much the same point, stating that years of hard work would be needed to get the law implemented.

> Just the sheer volume of regulations that agencies must issue and enforce and the number of new programs and payment systems they must create and test is reason enough to raise questions about how they can get the job done. And as with any law, the agencies have wide latitude in the implementation. In fact, most prominent among the complaints from critics of the overhaul is the degree of discretion handed to Health and Human Services Secretary Kathleen Sebelius and to multiple divisions in her department. That's not to mention agencies ranging from the Department of Labor to the Internal Revenue Service, which will decide exactly how to implement the law's many provisions.[4]

This Report

This report identifies provisions in PPACA that require, permit, or contemplate rulemaking by federal agencies to implement the legislation. To identify these provisions, CRS first searched through the text of the enrolled version of H.R. 3590 as passed by the House of Representatives and the Senate (because the text of the public law was not yet available) using a variety of terms ("regulation," "rule," "rulemaking," and "regulatory"). CRS also searched through the text of H.R. 4872, the Health Care and Education Reconciliation Act of 2010 (P.L. 111-152, March 30, 2010), which made a number of health-related financing and revenue changes to PPACA. [5] (Hereafter, "PPACA" will refer to PPACA as amended by the reconciliation act.) Although these searches identified more than 40 regulatory provisions in PPACA, it is unclear whether they identified all such provisions in the act. (See the Appendix of this report for a table listing these provisions.)

Where new regulations are required in PPACA, this report also describes provisions in the act that prescribe the substance of certain regulations, procedural requirements regarding the development of those rules, and provisions that establish regulatory deadlines. The report concludes with some observations regarding congressional delegations of authority to regulatory agencies and opportunities for congressional oversight of these health care regulations. In brief, the report indicates that (1) many policy decisions are still to be decided in forthcoming regulations that are explicitly required or permitted in PPACA; (2) the manner in which Congress requires or permits rulemaking can determine who makes those decisions, and in what manner; and (3) while the regulations are being developed by executive branch agencies, or after they are issued, Congress has various oversight options.

Some of the regulations that PPACA requires or permits have already been issued.[6] Other rules are expected to be issued in the coming months.[7] Still other PPACA-related rules may not be issued for years.

MANDATORY REGULATIONS

A number of provisions in PPACA specifically require federal agencies to issue regulations that define certain terms, establish substantive requirements, create certain programs, and determine the timing of particular events. Because the legislation specifically requires these actions to be implemented through regulations, federal agencies must take action and have no discretion to use other, non-regulatory techniques (e.g., adjudication, guidance documents, policy statements, letters, or memoranda). The mandatory regulatory provisions in PPACA include the following:

- Section 1001 of the legislation amended Part A of Title XXVII of the Public Health Service Act (PHSA, 42 U.S.C. §300gg et seq.) and created several new sections of that act.
- Subsection (a) of the new Section 2714 in the PHSA ("Extension of Dependent Coverage") states that a "group health plan and a health insurance issuer offering group or individual health insurance coverage that provides dependent coverage of children shall continue to make such coverage available for an adult child (who is not married) until the child turns 26 years of age." Subsection (b) then states that "The Secretary shall promulgate regulations to define dependents to which coverage shall be made available under subsection (a)."[8]
- Subsection (g) of the new Section 2715 of the PHSA ("Development and Utilization of Uniform Explanation of Coverage Documents and Standardized Definitions") states that "The Secretary shall, by regulation, provide for the development of standards for the definitions of terms used in health insurance coverage," including such insurance-related terms as "premium," "deductible," "co-insurance," "co-payment," and "preferred provider;" and such medical terms as "hospitalization," "hospital outpatient care," "physician services," "skilled nursing care," and "rehabilitation services."
- Subsection (b) of the new Section 2718 of the PHSA ("Bringing Down the Cost of Health Care Coverage") states that a health

insurance issuer offering group or individual health insurance coverage must provide an annual rebate to each enrollee under such coverage if the ratio of the amount of premium revenue expended by the issuer on certain costs to the total amount of premium revenue is less than certain levels. Paragraph (3) of that subsection states "The Secretary shall promulgate regulations for enforcing the provisions of this section and may provide for appropriate penalties."

- Section 1201 of PPACA also amended the PHSA, creating several new sections. One of the new sections, Section 2702 ("Guaranteed Availability of Coverage") generally requires each health insurance issuer that offers coverage (beginning in 2014) in the individual or group market in a state to accept every employer and individual in the state that applies for such coverage. Subsections 2702(b)(1) and (2) allow issuers to restrict enrollment to open and special enrollment periods, and to establish special enrollment periods for qualifying events. Subsection 2702(b)(3) states "The Secretary shall promulgate regulations with respect to enrollment periods under paragraphs (1) and (2)."
- Section 3001 of PPACA ("Hospital Value-Based Purchasing Program") adds a new subsection to Section 1886 of the Social Security Act (42 U.S.C. §1301 et seq.) that requires the Secretary to establish a hospital value-based purchasing program under which incentive payments are made to hospitals that meet certain performance standards. Paragraph (12) of the new subsection states that the Secretary "shall promulgate regulations to carry out the Program," and says the regulations should include the selection of performance measures, the methodology used to calculate hospitals' performance scores, and the methodology used to determine the amount of value-based incentive payments.
- Section 6402 of the act ("Enhanced Medicare and Medicaid Program Integrity Provisions") added a new Section 1128J to the Social Security Act. Subsection (h)(1) of that new section amends Section 1862 of the Social Security Act (at 42 U.S.C. §1395y) by adding a new section regarding Medicare on "Suspension of Payments Pending Investigation of Credible Allegations of Fraud." Among other things, the subsection states that "The Secretary shall promulgate regulations to carry out this subsection."
- Section 9023 of the act ("Qualifying Therapeutic Discovery Project Credit") adds a new section to the Internal Revenue Code of 1986

> stating, in part, that the Secretary shall "provide a grant to each person who makes a qualified investment in a qualifying therapeutic discovery project in the amount of 50 percent of such investment. No grant shall be made under this subsection with respect to any investment unless such investment is made during a taxable year beginning in 2009 or 2010." In establishing the time for payment of such grants, for investments of an ongoing nature, "the Secretary shall issue regulations to determine the date on which a qualified investment shall be deemed to have been made for purposes of this paragraph."

Also, in the Health Care and Education Reconciliation Act of 2010 that amended PPACA, Section 1409 ("Codification of Economic Substance Doctrine and Penalties") amended Section 7701 of the Internal Revenue Code of 1986 by inserting a new subsection stating, in part, that the "Secretary shall issue regulations requiring foreign taxes to be treated as expenses in determining pre-tax profit in appropriate cases."

Substantive Rulemaking Requirements

Many of the rulemaking requirements in PPACA give federal agencies substantial discretion in crafting the regulatory provisions that are required or permitted. For example, the previously mentioned requirement in Section 1001 of the act that the Secretary promulgate regulations defining "dependents" to which coverage shall be made available does not constrain the Secretary in any way in the development of those regulations. However, other parts of PPACA stipulate that the required regulations include certain substantive elements. For example:

- Subsection (c) of Section 1311 of PPACA ("Affordable Choices of Health Benefit Plans") states that "The Secretary shall, by regulation, establish criteria for the certification of health plans as qualified health plans." It goes on to say that the criteria must require that such plans meet eight minimum requirements (e.g., not employ marketing practices that discourage enrollment; ensure a sufficient choice of providers; include health plan networks that serve predominately low-income, medically underserved individuals; and utilize a standard format to present heath benefits plan options).

- Section 1332 of PPACA ("Waiver for State Innovation") permits states to apply to the Secretary for a waiver of any or all requirements of the section for plan years beginning on or after January 1, 2017. Subsection (a)(4)(B) of Section 1332 requires the Secretary to promulgate regulations relating to these state waivers. That subsection goes on to stipulate that the regulations provide processes (1) for public notice and comment at the state level, (2) that ensure the disclosure of the provisions of state law that the state seeks to waive and how the state will ensure compliance with certain other requirements in PPACA, (3) for providing public notice and comment after the application is received by the Secretary, (4) for the state to provide periodic reports to the Secretary regarding implementation of the program under the waiver, and (5) for the periodic evaluation of the program under the waiver by the Secretary.
- Section 2402 of the act ("Removal of Barriers to Providing Home and Community-Based Services") requires the Secretary of Health and Human Services to promulgate regulations to ensure that all states develop service systems that are designed to (1) "allocate resources for services in a manner that is responsive to the changing needs and choices of beneficiaries receiving noninstitutionally-based long-term services and supports (including such services and supports that are provided under programs other the State Medicaid program), and that provides strategies for beneficiaries receiving such services to maximize their independence, including through the use of client-employed providers"; (2) "provide the support and coordination needed for a beneficiary in need of such services (and their family caregivers or representative, if applicable) to design an individualized, self-directed, community-supported life"; and (3) "improve coordination among, and the regulation of, all providers of such services under federally and State-funded programs."
- Section 2702 of PPACA ("Payment Adjustment for Health-Acquired Conditions") requires the Secretary of Health and Human Services to identify in regulations the state practices applicable to the Medicaid program that prohibit payment for health-care acquired conditions. It also says that the regulations "shall prohibit payments to States under section 1903 of the Social Security Act for any amounts expended for providing medical assistance for health care-acquired conditions specified in the regulations. The regulations shall ensure that the prohibition on payment for health care-acquired conditions shall not

result in a loss of access to care or services for Medicaid beneficiaries."

- Subsection (b) of Section 4205 of the act ("Nutrition Labeling of Standard Menu Items at Chain Restaurants") amends Section 403(q)(5) of the Federal Food, Drug, and Cosmetic Act (21 U.S.C. §343(q)(5)) by adding a new provision on "Restaurants, Retail Food Establishments, and Vending Machines." Among other things, the new provision generally requires restaurants and retail food establishments to disclose on menus and menu boards (including a drive-through menu board) "a succinct statement concerning suggested daily caloric intake, as specified by the Secretary by regulation." The provision also says that this disclosure should be done "in a clear and conspicuous manner." Also, the provision states that the "Secretary shall establish by regulation standards for determining and disclosing the nutrient content for standard menu items that come in different flavors, varieties, or combinations, but which are listed as a single menu item, such as soft drinks, ice cream, pizza, doughnuts, or children's combination meals, through means determined by the Secretary, including ranges, averages, or other methods." In promulgating regulations in this section, the Secretary is required to "consider standardization of recipes and methods of preparation, reasonable variation in serving size and formulation of menu items, space on menus and menu boards, inadvertent human error, training of food service workers, variations in ingredients, and other factors, as the Secretary determines."

Procedural Requirements

During the past 65 years, Congress and various Presidents have developed an elaborate set of procedures and requirements to guide the federal rulemaking process, including the Administrative Procedure Act (APA, 5 U.S.C. §551 et seq.), the Regulatory Flexibility Act, the Paperwork Reduction Act, the Unfunded Mandates Reform Act, and Executive Order 12866.[9] For example, Section 553 of the APA generally requires that agencies publish a notice of proposed rulemaking in the *Federal Register*, allow "interested persons" an opportunity to comment on the proposed rule, and then publish the final rule, which generally cannot take effect for at least 30 days.[10] In addition to these crosscutting rulemaking requirements, certain statutes require that particular procedures be followed in the development of rules under those statutes.

Some of the mandatory regulatory provisions in PPACA stipulate that certain consultative or rulemaking procedures be followed in developing the required rules. For example:

- Subsection (b)(2) of Section 1104 of PPACA ("Administrative Simplification") amends Section 1173 of the Social Security Act (at 42 U.S.C. 1320d-2) and states, in part, that "The Secretary shall adopt operating rules under this subsection, by regulation." In developing those rules, the subsection requires consideration of operating rules developed by a non-profit entity described in a previous subparagraph, and the recommendation that is required to be submitted by the National Committee on Vital Health Statistics. Finally, the subsection states that the Secretary "shall promulgate an interim final rule applying any standard or operating rule recommended by the National Committee on Vital and Health Statistics," and "shall accept and consider public comments on any interim final rule published under this subparagraph for 60 days after the date of such publication."[11]
- Subsection (b)(2) of Section 1104 of the act also added a new subsection to Section 1173 of the Social Security Act concerning the review and amendment of the above-mentioned operating rules. It requires the Secretary to establish a review committee by January 1, 2014, with the committee's first report due by July 1, 2014, providing recommendations for updating and improving the operating rules. The subsection states that "Any recommendations to amend adopted standards and operating rules that have been approved by the review committee and reported to the Secretary under paragraph (2)(B) shall be adopted by the Secretary through promulgation of an interim final rule not later than 90 days after receipt of the committee's report."
- Subsection (a)(1) of Section 1321 of the act ("State Flexibility in Operation and Enforcement of Exchanges and Related Requirements") requires the Secretary to issue regulations setting standards for meeting the requirements Title I of PPACA "as soon as practicable after the date of enactment of this Act." In doing so, subsection (a)(2) requires the Secretary to consult with the National Association of Insurance Commissioners and its members, and with health insurance issuers, consumer organizations, and "such other

individuals as the Secretary selects in a manner designed to ensure balanced representation among interested parties."

- Section 1333 of PPACA ("Provisions Relating to Offering of Plans in More than One State") requires the Secretary to issue regulations for the creation of health care choice compacts (under which two or more states may enter into certain agreements) "in consultation with the National Association of Insurance Commissioners."
- Section 3307 of the act ("Improving Formulary Requirements for Prescription Drug Plans") amends the Social Security Act to require the Secretary to identify "categories and classes of drugs for which the Secretary determines are of clinical concern." Prior to making that determination, the Secretary is required to establish the criteria to be used "through the promulgation of a regulation which includes a public notice and comment period."
- Section 8002 of the act ("Establishment of a National Voluntary Insurance Program for Purchasing Community Living Assistance Services and Support") amended the PHSA by, among other things, adding a new Section 3203 ("CLASS Independence Benefit Plan") that requires the Secretary to develop at least three "actuarially sound benefit plans as alternatives for consideration for designation by the Secretary as the CLASS Independence Benefit Plan under which eligible beneficiaries shall receive benefits under this title." Subsection (a)(2) of this new section requires a "CLASS Independence Advisory Council" to evaluate the alternative plans and recommend the one that "best balances price and benefits to meet enrollee's needs in an actuarially sound manner." Using this information, Subsection (a)(3) requires the Secretary to designate a benefit plan as the CLASS Independence Benefit Plan, and to do so "along with details of the plan and the reasons for the selection by the Secretary, in a final rule that allows for a period of public comment."

Negotiated Rulemaking

One particularly notable procedural requirement is in Section 5602 of PPACA, which requires the Secretary of Health and Human Services to use a process called "negotiated rulemaking" to establish a "comprehensive methodology and criteria for designation of ... (A) medically underserved populations in accordance with section 330(b)(3) of the Public Health Service Act (42 U.S.C. §254b(b)(3))," and "(B) health professions shortage areas under section 332 of the Public Health Service Act (42 U.S.C. §254e)." In negotiated rulemaking, representatives of federal agencies and affected parties work together in a committee to reach consensus on what can ultimately become a proposed rule. Although negotiated rulemaking is not appropriate for all regulations, advocates believe that the approach can speed rule development, reduce litigation, and generate more creative and effective regulatory solutions.[12]

Section 5602 requires the Secretary to publish a notice in the *Federal Register* announcing the intention to form a negotiated rulemaking committee "not later than 45 days after the date of the enactment of this Act." As part of that notice, the target date for publication of the rule was required to be July 1, 2010. The negotiated rulemaking committee is required to be appointed not later than 30 days after the end of the comment period of the notice, and the facilitator of the committee is required to be appointed within 10 days after the committee is appointed. A preliminary committee report was required by April 1, 2010, with a final report required "not later than one month before the target publication date" (i.e., by June 1, 2010). The Secretary is required to publish an interim final rule by the target date, with a 90-day public comment period to follow. After considering those comments, the Secretary is to publish a final rule not later than one year after the target date.

Deadlines for the Development or Implementation of Rules

Many of the mandatory regulatory provisions in PPACA do not stipulate when the regulations must be issued or take effect. However, several provisions require the development or implementation of regulations within particular time frames or by particular dates. For example:

- As noted previously in this report, Section 1001 of PPACA amended Part A of Title XXVII of the Public Health Service Act (42 U.S.C. §300gg et seq.) and created several new sections of that act. Subsection (a) of the new Section 2717 ("Ensuring the Quality of Care") requires the Secretary to develop quality reporting requirements with respect to plan or coverage benefits and health care provider reimbursement structures. Subsection 2717(c) states that "Not later than 2 years after the date of enactment of the Patient Protection and Affordable Care Act, the Secretary shall promulgate regulations that provide criteria for determining whether a reimbursement structure is described in subsection (a).”

- Subsection (c) of Section 1104 of the act (“Administrative Simplification”) establishes specific dates by which three final rules are to be issued or effective. A final rule establishing a unique health plan identifier must be in effect by October 1, 2012. A final rule establishing a standard for electronic funds transfers must be adopted by January 1, 2012, and must be effective by January 1, 2014. A final rule to establish a transaction standard and a single set of associated operating rules for health claims attachments by January 1, 2014, and those rules must be in effect by January 1, 2016. Also, subsection 1104(b) requires that certain recommendations to amend adopted standards and operating rules be adopted through promulgation of an interim final rule within 90 days after receipt of a committee report.
- Subsection (l) of Section 1303 of the act (“Special Rules”) amends Section 1322(b) of PPACA (“Loans and Grants Under the CO-OP Program”) by adding a new paragraph stating, in part, “Not later than July 1, 2013, and prior to awarding loans and grants under the CO-OP program, the Secretary shall promulgate regulations with respect to the repayment of such loans and grants in a manner that is consistent with State solvency regulations and other similar State laws that may apply.”
- As noted previously in this report, Section 1332 of PPACA (“Waiver for State Innovation”) permits states to apply to the Secretary for a waiver of any or all requirements of the section for plan years beginning on or after January 1, 2017. Subsection 1332(a)(4)(B) requires the Secretary to promulgate regulations relating to such waivers “Not later than 180 days after the date of enactment of this Act.”
- Section 1333 of the act (“Provisions Relating to Offering of Plans in More than One State”) requires the Secretary to issue regulations by July 1, 2013, for the creation of health care choice compacts (under which two or more states may enter into certain agreements).
- Section 2702 of the act (“Payment Adjustment for Health Care-Acquired Conditions”) requires the Secretary of Health and Human Services to identify in regulations the state practices applicable to the Medicaid program that prohibit payment for health-care acquired conditions. It goes on to require that the regulations “be effective as of July 1, 2011.”

- Section 3007 of PPACA ("Value-Based Payment Modifier Under the Physician Fee Schedule") added a new subsection to Section 1848 of the Social Security Act (at 42 U.S.C. §1395w-4). Subparagraph (p)(4)(B)(i) of that new subsection states that "Subject to the preceding provisions of this subparagraph, the Secretary shall begin implementing the payment modifier established under this subsection through the rulemaking process during 2013 for the physician fee schedule established under subsection (b)."
- Subsection (b) of Section 4205 of the act ("Nutrition Labeling of Standard Menu Items at Chain Restaurants") amends Section 403(q)(5) of the Federal Food, Drug, and Cosmetic Act (21 U.S.C. §343(q)(5)) by adding a new provision on "Restaurants, Retail Food Establishments, and Vending Machines." Paragraph (x) of the new provision requires the Secretary to promulgate proposed regulations to carry out the clause "not later than 1 year after the date of enactment of this clause."
- Subsection (i) of Section 10201 of PPACA ("Amendments to the Social Security Act and Title II of This Act") amends Section 1115 of the Social Security Act (at 42 U.S.C. §1315) by adding a new subsection (d). Paragraph (2) of that subsection states that "Not later than 180 days after the date of enactment of this subsection, the Secretary shall promulgate regulations relating to applications for, and renewals of, a demonstration project"
- Subsection (l) of Section 10501 of the act ("Amendments to the Public Health Service Act, the Social Security Act, and Title V of This Act") adds a new subpart on "Training in Underserved Communities," and requires the Secretary to establish a grant program to (among other things) assist in the recruitment of students from underserved rural communities. Paragraph (f) of this new subpart states "Not later than 60 days after the date of enactment of this section, the Secretary shall by regulation define 'underserved rural community' for the purposes of this section."

In some of the provisions, PPACA provides only general time constraints on rulemaking. For example, Section 1321 of the act ("State Flexibility in Operation and Enforcement of Exchanges and Related Requirements") states that the Secretary shall issue regulations setting standards for meeting the requirements under this title "as soon as practicable after the date of enactment of this Act."

One provision in PPACA prohibits the development of regulations until a particular date. Subsection (a)(6)(D) of Section 3132 ("Hospice Reform") states that "not earlier than October 1, 2013, the Secretary shall, by regulation, implement revisions to the methodology for determining the payment rates for routine home care and other services included in hospice care under this part, as the Secretary determines to be appropriate."

DISCRETIONARY REGULATIONS

Other provisions in PPACA permit, but do not require, federal agencies to issue certain regulations. The amount of discretion provided to the agencies appears to vary with the wording of each provision, as do the implications of that discretion. In some cases, the agencies may be able to decide whether to take any action, and if so, whether that action takes the form of a regulation or some other method of policy implementation (e.g., adjudication, policy statements, guidance documents, or memoranda). As Jeffrey Lubbers noted in *A Guide to Federal Agency Rulemaking*,

> It is accepted that agencies are generally free to decide whether to formulate policy through rulemaking or adjudication.... Apart from rulemaking and adjudication, there are, of course, a variety of informal means by which administrative agencies articulate policy under a statute. Among these are press releases, speeches, statements, letters, advisory opinions, rulings, negotiation and litigation strategies, and a host of other types of communications. The extent to which these informal means of articulating policy are binding on the public will vary, but their binding effect usually will be significantly less than that of a "rule" issued after rulemaking or an "order" after adjudication.[13]

He also said that congressional authorization to "make such rules and regulations as may be necessary ... clearly enables an agency to promulgate procedural, organizational, or other 'housekeeping' rules and probably also enables an agency to issue nonbinding guidelines or interpretations of its statutory mandate."[14]

Provisions in PPACA that give agencies discretion in whether to issue regulations (as opposed to guidelines or other methods that are not specifically regulations) include the following:

- Subsection (d)(2)(B) of Section 1302 of PPACA ("Essential Health Benefits Requirements") states that "The Secretary may issue regulations under which employer contributions to a health savings account (within the meaning of section 223 of the Internal Revenue Code of 1986) may be taken into account in determining the level of coverage for a plan of the employer." Given the language of this subsection ("may issue regulations"), the Secretary appears to be allowed to take no action regarding employer contributions. If the Secretary elects to act, it is unclear whether the Secretary must do so through regulations, or whether the contributions can be allowed to be taken into account in other, non-regulatory ways (e.g., through some type of non-binding implementing guidance).
- Subsection (h) of Section 1311 of the act ("Affordable Choices of Health Benefit Plans") states that, beginning on January 1, 2015, a qualified health plan may contract with a health care provider "only if such provider implements such mechanisms to improve health care quality as the Secretary may by regulation require." Given this wording, the Secretary appears to be allowed not to require such improvement mechanisms. If the Secretary decides to require mechanisms to improve health care quality, it is unclear whether this subsection requires the Secretary to do so through regulations or whether other, non-regulatory methods can be used.
- Another provision in subsection (h) of Section 1311 (paragraph (1)(A)) places restrictions on contracts with hospitals greater than 50 beds, but goes on to say that the Secretary "may by regulation adjust the number of beds described in paragraph (1)(A)." This language appears to allow the Secretary not to take any action (thereby keeping the number of beds at 50). On the other hand, if the Secretary decides to adjust the number of beds, it is unclear whether the language in this subsection requires the Secretary to do so by issuing a regulation.
- Subsection (h) of Section 1322 of the act ("Federal Program to Assist Establishment and Operation of Nonprofit, Member-Run Health Insurance Issuers") amends Section 501(c) of the Internal Revenue Code of 1986 adding "Co-Op Health Insurance Issuers" to the list of exempt organizations. The subsection goes on to say that the exemption applies only if the organization has "given notice to the Secretary, in such manner as the Secretary may by regulations prescribe, that it is applying for recognition of its status under this paragraph." Given this construction, the Secretary arguably may

decide not to specify the manner of notice. However, if the Secretary does elect to do so, it is unclear whether this subsection requires that the manner of notice be prescribed in a regulation.

- Section 1401 of the act ("Refundable Tax Credit Providing Premium Assistance for Coverage Under a Qualified Health Plan") amended the Internal Revenue Code of 1986 and added a new Section 36B on "Refundable Credit for Coverage Under a Qualified Health Plan." Subsection (g) of this new section states that "The Secretary shall prescribe such regulations as may be necessary to carry out the provisions of this section." Given this language, the Secretary may conclude that regulations are not needed to accomplish the objectives of the new Section 36B. It is unclear from this language whether other, non-regulatory methods are available.
- Section 1513 of PPACA ("Shared Responsibility for Employers") amends Chapter 43 of the Internal Revenue Code of 1986 by adding a new Section 4980H on "Shared Responsibility for Employers Regarding Health Coverage." Subsection (3) of that section states that the "Secretary shall prescribe rules, regulations, or guidance for the repayment of any assessable payment (including interest) if such payment is based on the allowance or payment of an applicable premium tax credit or cost-sharing reduction with respect to an employee, such allowance or payment is subsequently disallowed, and the assessable payment would not have been required to be made but for such allowance or payment." Assuming that the latter conditions are met, this subsection appears to require the Secretary to take some type of action. However, the "rules, regulations, or guidance" language suggests that any of those mechanisms would satisfy the statutory requirement, not just regulations.
- Section 1557 of PPACA ("Nondiscrimination") prohibits the exclusion of an individual from participation, denial of benefits, or other forms of discrimination regarding any covered health program or activity. Subsection (c) states that the "Secretary may promulgate regulations to implement this section." Given this language, the Secretary arguably may conclude that the section can be implemented without regulations. However, if the Secretary decides to act, it is unclear whether non-regulatory methods can be used to implement the section.
- Section 3507 of the act ("Presentation of Prescription Drug Benefit and Risk Information") requires the Secretary to submit a report to

Congress no later than one year after the date of enactment of PPACA determining whether the addition of quantitative summaries of the benefits and risks of prescription drugs in a standardized format to promotional labeling or print advertising would improve health care decision making by clinicians, patients, and consumers. If the Secretary determines in that report that quantitative summaries are needed, then the Secretary is required to promulgate "proposed regulations as necessary" to implement that format within three years after the date that the report is submitted. On the other hand, if the Secretary determines that quantitative summaries are not needed, then no proposed rule need be developed.

- Subsection (a) of Section 6401 of the act ("Provider Screening and Other Enrollment Requirements Under Medicare, Medicaid, and CHIP") amends Section 1866(j) of the Social Security Act (at 42 U.S.C. 1395cc(j)) and requires the Secretary to establish procedures under which screening is conducted with respect to providers of medical or other items or services "not later than 180 days after the date of enactment of this paragraph." Subsections (B) through (D) describe the level of screening to be conducted, application fees, and application and enforcement provisions. Finally, subsection (E) states that "The Secretary may promulgate an interim final rule to carry out this paragraph." Given this discretionary language, the Secretary appears able to conclude that regulations are not needed. If a regulatory approach is used, the Secretary may use regular notice and comment rulemaking, or may issue an interim final rule (which typically take effect immediately with a post-promulgation opportunity for public comment).

Also, Section 3014 of PPACA ("Quality Measurement") amends the Social Security Act (at 42 U.S.C. §1395aaa(b)) to require the Secretary to "establish a pre-rulemaking process" under which certain steps occur regarding the selection of quality measures. Among other things, the amendment requires the Secretary to (1) make a list of quality measures being considered available to the public by December 1 of each year (beginning with 2011); (2) be provided with input from stakeholder groups by February 1 of each year (beginning with 2012); and (3) assess the quality impact of certain measures by March 1, 2012, and at least once every three years thereafter. Notably, however, this "pre-rulemaking process" is not specifically required to result in a regulation.

OTHER REGULATORY PROVISIONS

In other sections of PPACA, the statutory language appears to contemplate the use of regulations to fulfill the underlying policy requirement, but the language does not specifically require or permit federal agencies to issue new regulations. One possibility is that these sections of the act refer to existing rules. If so, new regulations may not be needed to satisfy the requirements in PPACA. However, to the extent that implementing regulations are not already in existence, new rules may need to be established, or existing rules may need to be amended. Examples of these kinds of provisions include the following:

- Subsection (b) of Section 1302 of PPACA ("Essential Health Benefits Requirements") generally requires the Secretary to "define the essential health benefits," but also says that they must include certain elements (e.g., emergency services, maternity and newborn care, and prescription drugs). Subsection (d) of this section describes four levels of coverage (bronze, silver, gold, and platinum), and also says "Under regulations issued by the Secretary, the level of coverage of a plan shall be determined on the basis that the essential health benefits described in subsection (b) shall be provided to a standard population (and without regard to the population the plan may actually provide benefits to)."
- Section 1511 of the act ("Automatic Enrollment for Employees of Large Employers") amends the Fair Labor Standards Act of 1938 (FLSA) by inserting a new Section 18A that states "In accordance with regulations promulgated by the Secretary, an employer to which this Act applies that has more than 200 full-time employees and that offers employees enrollment in 1 or more health benefits plans shall automatically enroll new full-time employees in one of the plans offered (subject to any waiting period authorized by law) and to continue the enrollment of current employees in a health benefits plan offered through the employer."
- Section 1512 of the act ("Employer Requirement to Inform Employees of Coverage Options") also amends the FLSA by inserting a new Section 18B stating "In accordance with regulations promulgated by the Secretary, an employer to which this Act applies, shall provide to each employee at the time of hiring (or with respect to current employees, not later than March 1, 2013), written notice" to

employees of the existence of an exchange, that the employee may be eligible for a tax credit and a cost sharing reduction, and that the employee will lose any employer contribution if the employee purchases a qualified health plan through the exchange.

- Section 3208 of the act ("Making Senior Housing Facility Demonstration Permanent") amends Section 1859 of the Social Security Act (at 42 U.S.C. §1395w-28) by adding a new section stating, in part, that the service area of a Medicare Advantage senior housing facility plan described in that section may be limited to a senior housing facility in a geographic area "in accordance with regulations of the Secretary."
- Subsection (b) of Section 6401 of the act ("Provider Screening and Other Enrollment Requirements Under Medicare, Medicaid, and CHIP") amends Section 1902(a) of the Social Security Act (at 42 U.S.C. §1396a(a)) to, among other things, add requirements for "Provider and Supplier Screening, Oversight, and Reporting." One of those requirements is that the state complies with the national system for reporting criminal and civil adverse provider actions to the Secretary "in accordance with regulations of the Secretary."
- Section 6402 of the act ("Enhanced Medicare and Medicaid Program Integrity Provisions") added a new Section 1128J to the Social Security Act. Subsection (h)(2) of Section 6402 requires the following: "by any individual or entity to whom the State has failed to suspend payments under the plan during any period when there is pending an investigation of a credible allegation of fraud against the individual or entity, as determined by the State in accordance with regulations promulgated by the Secretary for purposes of section 1862(o) and this subparagraph, unless the State determines in accordance with such regulations there is good cause not to suspend such payments."
- Subsection (d) of Section 10108 of the act ("Free Choice Vouchers") states that "The cost of any health plan shall be determined under the rules similar to the rules of section 2204 of the Public Health Service Act, except that such amount shall be adjusted for age and category of enrollment in accordance with regulations established by the Secretary."

The previous sections of this report illustrate that PPACA gives federal agencies substantial responsibility and authority to "fill in the details" of the legislation through subsequent regulations.

CONCLUSION

The first of these implementing regulations were due in 2010, but some are not required to be promulgated or take effect until much later. These regulatory requirements are also likely to be reviewed and revised as agencies gain experience in implementing the statute. In addition, federal agencies are also likely to issue clarifying or implementing regulations regarding particular provisions in the act, even though the act does not specifically require or authorize them to do so.[15] Therefore, it seems likely that there will be a great deal of regulatory activity relating to the many provisions in PPACA for years, or even decades to come.

As Henry J. Aaron and Robert D. Reischauer noted in their article entitled "The War Isn't Over," many of the regulations developed pursuant to the provisions in PPACA will likely "provoke controversy."[16] Some of these controversies are likely to center on the contents of the rules that are developed (e.g., how the Secretary defines "dependents" to whom coverage is required to be made available pursuant to subsection (a) of Section 2714 of the act). Other controversies may focus on whether the agencies have satisfied the procedural requirements specified in PPACA, or the requirements in the myriad of other statutes and executive orders that determine the federal rulemaking process. Still other controversies may arise regarding whether federal agencies need to issue regulations in discretionary areas at all.

Wording of Regulatory Provisions Matters

Congress can assign regulatory responsibilities to federal agencies in any number of ways, but the manner by which Congress does so can determine the amount of discretion given to the agencies and, conversely, the amount of control that Congress retains for itself. When Congress requires that a regulation be issued or made effective by a particular date, that it contain certain substantive elements, and that the rule be developed following certain procedures, then the delegation of legislative rulemaking authority is somewhat limited and Congress retains a measure of control over the subsequent policymaking process. On the other hand, Congress grants substantial discretion to the regulatory agencies when it gives the heads of those agencies broad authority to "prescribe such regulations as may be necessary." Even more discretion may be given to the agencies when Congress permits agencies to decide certain threshold issues. For example, subsection (d)(2)(B) of Section 1302 of PPACA states that "The Secretary may issue regulations under which employer contributions to a health savings account ... may be taken into account in determining the level of coverage for a plan of the employer." Therefore, the Secretary arguably may decide not to take any actions to allow those contributions to be taken into account. Some observers of the rulemaking process have previously expressed concerns that Congress often gives too much discretion to regulatory agencies.[17]

Congressional delegations of authority to rulemaking agencies may be necessary because Congress does not have the technical knowledge needed to legislate within particular areas, or because Congress cannot reach consensus on how particular issues should be resolved. Giving regulatory agencies discretion to decide how certain rules should be crafted can allow them to devise approaches that will yield the desired outcomes at the lowest costs.

Conversely, constraining the agencies with unrealistic deadlines or with extremely detailed substantive requirements in statutes can result in rules that cost more than the benefits that they are expected to provide.[18] Some regulatory observers have previously expressed concerns that congressional delegations of rulemaking authority are sometimes too specific.[19] Also, the Government Accountability Office (GAO) concluded in 1999 that some regulatory provisions that were considered burdensome by private sector companies were directly traceable to specific statutory requirements.[20]

Also, several of the procedural requirements in PPACA are likely to affect the degree to which the public is able to participate in the rulemaking process. For example, several provisions in the act require or permit federal agencies to issue interim final rules instead of going through the public notice and comment process. Although interim final rulemaking may speed the issuance of the associated regulation, doing so may not allow the public to comment before the rule becomes final.

In addition, public participation may be limited when agencies are allowed to implement certain provisions through non-binding guidance or other non-regulatory mechanisms. In contrast, other provisions in PPACA specifically require notice and comment rulemaking, consultation with affected parties before a proposed rule is developed, comment periods after rules are published, or some combination of these requirements.

Regardless of whether congressional delegations of regulatory authority are broad or specific, Congress has a range of tools available to oversee the rules that federal agencies are expected to issue to implement PPACA, including oversight hearings and confirmation hearings for the heads of regulatory agencies.

Congressional Oversight Options

Individual Members of Congress may also participate in the rulemaking process by, among other things, meeting with agency officials and filing public comments.[21] As one author indicated,

> [I]nvestigations conducted by congressional committees constitute another powerful device of formal political supervision.... The public legislative hearings, in which administrative action is carefully scrutinized and a commissioner or staff member is plied with questions, symbolizes the unparalleled sophistication of American congressional control over administrative action, in general and by [independent regulatory agencies], in particular. Individual oversight by representatives or senators also takes place. Through correspondence or meetings, the latter convey the concerns of their constituents.[22]

Another option is the Congressional Review Act (CRA, 5 U.S.C. §§801-808)), which was enacted in 1996 in an attempt to reestablish a measure of congressional authority over rulemaking "without at the same time requiring Congress to become a super regulatory agency."[23] The act generally requires federal agencies to submit all of their covered final rules to both houses of Congress and GAO before they can take effect.[24] It also established expedited legislative procedures (primarily in the Senate) by which Congress may disapprove agencies' final rules by enacting a joint resolution of disapproval.[25] The definition of a covered rule in the CRA is quite broad, arguably including any type of document (e.g., legislative rules, policy statements, guidance, manuals, and memoranda) that the agency wishes to make binding on the affected public.[26] After these rules are submitted, Congress can use the expedited procedures specified in the CRA (particularly in the Senate) to disapprove any of the rules. CRA resolutions of disapproval must be presented to the President for signature or veto.

For a variety of reasons, however, the CRA has been used to disapprove only one rule in the 14 years since it was enacted.[27] Perhaps most notably, it is likely that a President would veto a resolution of disapproval to protect rules developed under his own administration, and it may be difficult for Congress to muster the two-thirds vote in both houses needed to overturn the veto.

APPENDIX. REGULATORY PROVISIONS IN PPACA

Table A-1. Regulatory Provisions in PPACA

Section of PPACA	Regulatory Provision	Regulatory Deadlines
Mandatory Regulations Section 1001 (creating a new Section 2714 of the Public Health Service Act (PHSA)	"The Secretary shall promulgate regulations to define dependents to which coverage shall be made available."	None
Section 1001 (creating a new Section 2715 of the PHSA)	"The Secretary shall, by regulation, provide for the development of standards for the definitions of terms used in health insurance coverage ... "	None
Section 1001 (creating a new Section 2717 of the PHSA)	" ... the Secretary shall promulgate regulations that provide criteria for determining whether a reimbursement structure is described in subsection (a)."	Promulgation of regulations within two years after the date of enactment (i.e., by March 23, 2012).
Section 1001 (creating a new Section 2718 of the PHSA)	"The Secretary shall promulgate regulations for enforcing the provisions of this section and may provide appropriate penalties."	None
Section 1104	"The Secretary shall adopt operating rules under this subsection, by regulation ... " and "shall promulgate an interim final rule applying any standard or operating rule recommended by the National Committee on Vital and Health Statistics."	Final rule to establish a unique health plan identifier must be effective by October 1, 2012. Final rule establishing a standard for electronic funds transfers must be adopted by January 1, 2012, and effective by January 1, 2014. Final rule to establish a transaction standard and single set of rules for health claims attachments by January 1, 2014, and in effect by January 1, 2016. Committee-recommended rules must be promulgated as interim final within 90 days of the committee's report.

Table A-1. (Continued)

Section of PPACA	Regulatory Provision	Regulatory Deadlines
Section 1201 (creating a new Section 2702 of the PHSA)	"The Secretary shall promulgate regulations with respect to enrollment periods under paragraphs (1) and (2)."	This section applies to enrollments starting in 2014.
Subsection 1303(l)	"... the Secretary shall promulgate regulations with respect to the repayment of such loans and grants ..."	Promulgation by July 1, 2013.
Subsection 1311(c)	"The Secretary shall, by regulation, establish criteria for the certification of health plans as qualified health plans."	None
Section 1321	"The Secretary shall ... issue regulations setting standards for meeting the requirements under this title, and the amendments made by this title, with respect to ..."	Promulgation "as soon as practicable after the date of enactment of this Act."
Subsection 1332(a)(4)(B)	"... the Secretary shall promulgate regulations relating to waivers under this section that provide ..."	Promulgation of rules within 180 days of enactment (i.e., by September 19, 2010).
Section 1333	"the Secretary shall ... issue regulations for the creation of health care choice compacts under which 2 or more States may enter into an agreement under which ..."	Regulations are to be issued by July 1, 2013.
Section 2402	"The Secretary of Health and Human Services shall promulgate regulations to ensure that all States develop service systems that are designed to ..."	None
Section 2702	"The Secretary of Health and Human Services ... shall identify current State practices that prohibit payment for health care-acquired conditions and shall incorporate the practices identified ... in regulations."	Regulations must be effective by July 1, 2011.
Section 3001	"The Secretary shall promulgate regulations to carry out the Program, including the selection of measures ... the methodology ... that is used to calculate hospital performance scores, and the methodology used to determine the amount of value-based incentive payments ..."	None

Section of PPACA	Regulatory Provision	Regulatory Deadlines
Section 3007	"... the Secretary shall begin implementing the payment modifier established under this subsection through the rulemaking process ..."	Implementation to begin during 2013.
Subsection 3132(a)(6)(D)	"... the Secretary shall, by regulation, implement revisions to the methodology for determining payment rates for routine home care and other services included in hospice care under this part ..."	Implementation not earlier than October 1, 2013.
Section 3307	"The Secretary shall establish the criteria under clause (ii)(II) and any exceptions under clause (i)(II) through the promulgation of a regulation which includes a public notice and comment period."	None (although the amendments in this section apply to plan years 2011 and beyond).
Subsection 4205(b)	"... statement concerning suggested daily caloric intake, as specified by the Secretary by regulation ..." and "the Secretary shall establish by regulation standards for determining and disclosing the nutrient content for standard menu items ..."	Promulgation of proposed regulations within one year of enactment (i.e., by March 23, 2011).
Section 5602	"The Secretary of Health and Human Services ... shall establish, through a negotiated rulemaking process...a comprehensive methodology and criteria for designation of (A) medically underserved populations ... [and](B) health professions shortage areas ..."	Target date for publication of the rule required to be July 1, 2010.
Section 6402 (adding a new Section 1128J to the Social Security Act)	"The Secretary shall promulgate regulations to carry out this subsection."	Requirements must be in effect by January 1, 2011.
Section 8002 (adding a new section 3203 to the PHSA)	"The Secretary shall publish such designation ... in a final rule that allows for a period of public comment."	Designation by October 1, 2012.
Section 9023	" ... the Secretary shall issue regulations to determine the date on which a qualified investment shall be deemed to have been made for purposes of this paragraph."	None
Subsection 10201(i)	" ... the Secretary shall promulgate regulations relating to applications for, and renewals of, a demonstration project ..."	Promulgation of the rule within 180 days after enactment (i.e., by September 19, 2010).
Subsection 10501(l)	"The Secretary shall by regulation define 'underserved rural community' for the purposes of this section."	Regulation required within 60 days after enactment (i.e., by May 22, 2010).

Table A-1. (Continued)

Section of PPACA	Regulatory Provision	Regulatory Deadlines
Section 1409 (Health Care and Education Reconciliation Act of 2010)	"The Secretary shall issue regulations requiring foreign taxes to be treated as expenses in determining pre-tax profit in appropriate cases."	None
Discretionary Regulations		
Subsection 1302(d)(2)(B)	"The Secretary may issue regulations under which employer contributions to a health savings account ... may be taken into account in determining the level of coverage for a plan of the employer."	None
Subsection 1311(h)	A qualified health plan may contract with a health care provider "only if such provider implements such mechanisms to improve health care quality as the Secretary may by regulation require." "The Secretary may by regulation adjust the number of beds described in paragraph (1)(A)."	None
Subsection 1322(h)	An exemption applies only if the organization has given notice to the Secretary "in such manner as the Secretary may by regulations prescribe, that it is applying for recognition of its status under this paragraph."	None
Section 1401	"The Secretary shall prescribe such regulations as may be necessary to carry out the provisions of this section ... "	None
Section 1513	"The Secretary shall prescribe rules, regulations, or guidance for the repayment of any assessable payment ... " if certain conditions are met.	None
Section 1557	"The Secretary may promulgate regulations to implement this section."	None
Section 3014	"The Secretary shall establish a pre-rulemaking process under which the following steps occur ... "	None

Section of PPACA	Regulatory Provision	Regulatory Deadlines
Section 3507	"If the Secretary determines... that the addition of quantitative summaries ... would improve health care decisionmaking ..., then the Secretary...shall promulgate proposed regulations as necessary to implement such format."	Promulgation of proposed rules within three years of the submission of a report (which is required by March 23, 2011).
Section 6401(a)	"The Secretary may promulgate an interim final rule to carry out this paragraph."	Procedures are required within 180 days after enactment (i.e., by September 19, 2010).
Other Regulatory Provisions		
Subsection 1302(b)	"Under regulations issued by the Secretary ... "	None
Section 1511	"In accordance with regulations promulgated by the Secretary ... "	None
Section 1512	"In accordance with regulations promulgated by the Secretary ... "	Substantive requirements must be implemented by March 1, 2013.
Section 3208	" ... in accordance with regulations of the Secretary."	None
Subsection 6401(b)	" ... in accordance with regulations of the Secretary."	None
Section 6402 (adding a new Section 1128J to the Social Security Act)	" ... in accordance with regulations promulgated by the Secretary ..."	None
Subsection 10108(d)	" ... in accordance with regulations established by the Secretary ..."	None

Source: CRS.

Congress can also use regular (i.e., non-CRA) legislative procedures to disapprove agencies' rules, but such legislation may prove even more difficult to enact than a CRA resolution of disapproval (primarily because of the lack of expedited procedures in the Senate), and if enacted may also be vetoed by the President.

Although the CRA has been used only once to overturn an agency rule, Congress has regularly included provisions in the text of agencies' appropriations bills directing or preventing the development of particular regulations. Such provisions include prohibitions on the finalization of particular proposed rules, restrictions on certain types of regulatory activity, and restrictions on implementation or enforcement of certain provisions.[28] Appropriations provisions can also be used to prompt agencies to issue certain regulations, or to require that certain procedures be followed before or after their issuance. The inclusion of regulatory provisions in appropriations legislation as a matter of legislative strategy appears to be prompted by two factors: (1) Congress's ability via its "power of the purse" to control agency action, and (2) the fact that appropriations bills are considered "must pass" legislation. Congress's use of regulatory appropriations restrictions has fluctuated somewhat over time, and previous experience suggests that they may be somewhat less frequent when Congress and the President are of the same party.[29]

End Notes

[1] David H. Rosenbloom, Building a Legislative-Centered Public Administration: Congress and the Administrative State, 1946-1999 (Tuscaloosa, AL: The University of Alabama Press, 2000), pp. 133-134.

[2] For more information on PPACA, see CRS Report R40942, Private Health Insurance Provisions in the Patient Protection and Affordable Care Act (PPACA), by Hinda Chaikind, Bernadette Fernandez, and Mark Newsom; CRS Report R40970, Medicare Program Changes in Senate-Passed H.R. 3590, coordinated by Patricia A. Davis; and CRS Report R41037, Medicaid and the Children's Health Insurance Program (CHIP) Provisions in H.R. 3590, as Passed by the Senate, by Evelyne P. Baumrucker et al..

[3] Henry J. Aaron and Robert D. Reischauer, "The War Isn't Over," New England Journal of Medicine, Health Care Reform Center, March 24, 2010, available at http://healthcarereform.nejm.org/?p=3223&query

[4] John Reichard, "Health: After the Win, No Time to Lose," CQ Weekly, April 5, 2010, p. 814, available at http://library.cqpress.com/cqweekly/document.php?id=weeklyreport111-000003636588&PHPSESSID= 7sgss0dfm1o1dtrkof8h2lvms5.

[5] For more information on the reconciliation legislation, see CRS Report R41124, Medicare: Changes Made by the Reconciliation Act of 2010 to the Patient Protection and

Affordable Care Act (P.L. 111-148), coordinated by Patricia A. Davis; CRS Report R41125, Medicaid and CHIP: Changes Made by the Health Care and Education Reconciliation Act of 2010 (HCERA, P.L. 111-152) to the Patient Protection and Affordable Care Act (PPACA, P.L. 111-148), coordinated by Evelyne P. Baumrucker and Cliff Binder; CRS Report R41126, Private Health Insurance: Changes Made by H.R. 4872, the Health Care and Education Reconciliation Act of 2010, by Hinda Chaikind et al.; and CRS Report R41128, Health-Related Revenue Provisions in the Patient Protection and Affordable Care Act (PPACA) , by Janemarie Mulvey.

[6] See CRS Report R41346, Initial Final Rules Implementing the Patient Protection and Affordable Care Act, by Curtis W. Copeland.

[7] See CRS Report R41586, Upcoming Rules Pursuant to the Patient Protection and Affordable Care Act, by Curtis W. Copeland and Maeve P. Carey.

[8] In most of these provisions, the "Secretary" referred to in PPACA appears to be the Secretary of Health and Human Services. In other cases (e.g., provisions that amend the Internal Revenue Code), the "Secretary" appears to be the Secretary of the Treasury.

[9] For a discussion of these and other rulemaking requirements, see CRS Report RL32240, The Federal Rulemaking Process: An Overview, by Curtis W. Copeland.

[10] The APA contains numerous exceptions to these general requirements. For example, the APA (5 U.S.C. §553(b)(3)(B)) states that the notice and comment procedures do not apply when the agency finds, for "good cause," that those procedures are "impracticable, unnecessary, or contrary to the public interest."

[11] In interim final rulemaking, the agency issues a final rule without a prior notice of proposed rulemaking. The interim final rule is generally effective immediately, but with a post-promulgation opportunity for the public to comment. If the public comments persuade the agency that changes are needed in the interim final rule, the agency may revise the rule by publishing a final rule reflecting those changes. For more information, see Michael Asimow, "Interim Final Rules: Making Haste Slowly, Administrative Law Review, 51 (Summer 1999), pp. 703-755.

[12] For more information, see CRS Report RL32452, Negotiated Rulemaking, by Curtis W. Copeland.

[13] Jeffrey S. Lubbers, A Guide to Federal Agency Rulemaking, 4th ed. (Chicago, IL: 2006), pp. 127-128.

[14] Ibid., p. 131.

[15] For example, on March 29, 2010, the Secretary of Health and Human Services told insurers that forthcoming regulations would "ensure that there is no ambiguity" that PPACA prohibits insurers from both denying an uninsured child coverage because of a pre-existing condition and denying treatments for an insured child's pre-existing condition beginning in September 2010. Sarah Barr, "Sebelius Says Regulations Will Clarify Rules on Pre-Existing Condition Denials for Children," BNA Daily Report for Executives, March 30, 2010, p. A-20.

[16] Henry J. Aaron and Robert D. Reischauer, "The War Isn't Over," New England Journal of Medicine, Health Care Reform Center, March 24, 2010, available at http://healthcarereform.nejm.org/?p=3223&query

[17] See, for example, David Schoenbrod, Power Without Responsibility: How Congress Abuses the People Through Delegation (New Haven: Yale University Press, 1993).

[18] For example, on January 15, 2010, the Federal Railroad Administration (FRA) within the Department of Transportation (DOT) published a final rule in the Federal Register defining criteria for "positive train control" systems that were required on certain passenger and

freight rail lines by the Rail Safety Improvement Act of 2008 (P.L. 110- 432, 122 Stat. 4854, October 16, 2008). (U.S. Department of Transportation, Federal Railroad Administration, "Positive Train Control Systems," 75 Federal Register 2598, January 15, 2010.) "Positive train control systems" refers to technology that can prevent accidents such as train-to-train collisions and train movements through a switch left in the wrong position. Congress enacted the statutory requirement in the wake of several serious rail accidents involving dozens of fatalities and hundreds of injuries. Although the rule was expected to reduce deaths and injuries by more than 50%, FRA estimated that the cost of the rule would be more than 20 times its estimated benefits. FRA noted this imbalance in the rule, but said it was "constrained by the requirements of [the Rail Safety Improvement Act of 2008], which do not provide latitude for implementing [positive train controls] differently" (p. 2685).

[19] See, for example, Committee for Economic Development, Modernizing Government Regulation: The Need for Action, April 1, 1998, available at http://www.ced.org/images

[20] U.S. Government Accountability Office, Regulatory Burden: Some Agencies' Claims Regarding Lack of Rulemaking Discretion Have Merit, GAO/GGD-99-20, January 8, 1999. GAO concluded that for 13 of 27 regulatory concerns that the businesses cited, the underlying statutes gave the rulemaking agencies no discretion in establishing the regulatory requirements at issue.

[21] In Sierra Club v. Costle (657 F.2d 298, D.C. Cir. 1981), the D.C. Circuit concluded (at 409) that it was "entirely proper for congressional representatives vigorously to represent the interests of their constituents before administrative agencies engaged in informal, general policy rulemaking, so long as the individual Members of Congress do not frustrate the intent of Congress as a whole as expressed in statute, nor undermine applicable rules of procedure."

[22] Dominique Custos, "The Rulemaking Power of Independent Regulatory Agencies," The American Journal of Comparative Law, vol. 54 (Fall 2006), p. 633.

[23] Joint statement of House and Senate Sponsors, 142 Cong. Rec. E571, at E571 (daily ed. April 19, 1996); 142 Cong. Rec. S3683, at S3683 (daily ed. April 18, 1996).

[24] If a rule is considered "major" (e.g., has a $100 million annual effect on the economy), then the CRA generally prohibits it from taking effect until 60 days after the date that it is submitted to Congress.

[25] For a detailed discussion of CRA procedures, see CRS Report RL31160, Disapproval of Regulations by Congress: Procedure Under the Congressional Review Act, by Richard S. Beth.

[26] For more on the potential scope of the definition of a "rule" under the CRA, see CRS Report RL30116, Congressional Review of Agency Rulemaking: An Update and Assessment of The Congressional Review Act after a Decade, by Morton Rosenberg.

[27] The rule overturned in March 2001 was the Occupational Safety and Health Administration's ergonomics standard. This reversal was the result of a unique set of circumstances in which the incoming President (George W. Bush) did not veto the resolution disapproving the outgoing President's (William J. Clinton's) rule. See CRS Report RL30116, Congressional Review of Agency Rulemaking: An Update and Assessment of The Congressional Review Act after a Decade, by Morton Rosenberg, for a description of several possible factors affecting the CRA's use, and for other effects that the act may have on agency rulemaking.

[28] See CRS Report RL34354, Congressional Influence on Rulemaking and Regulation Through Appropriations Restrictions, by Curtis W. Copeland.

[29] Ibid., p. 35. This report indicated that some appropriations restrictions were repeated every year for 10 years, some were repeated several years in a row but then stopped, and some appeared in only one appropriations bill. Some restrictions appeared to be intended to stop particular rules issued at the end of presidential administrations.

In: Rules and Rulemaking in the Patient... ISBN: 978-1-61942-194-3
Editors: Raphael Kipp and Vince Caputo © 2012 Nova Science Publishers, Inc

Chapter 2

UPCOMING RULES PURSUANT TO THE PATIENT PROTECTION AND AFFORDABLE CARE ACT: SPRING 2011 UNIFIED AGENDA*

Maeve P. Carey and Curtis W. Copeland

SUMMARY

Congress delegates rulemaking authority to agencies for a variety of reasons and in a variety of ways. The Patient Protection and Affordable Care Act (PPACA; P.L. 111-148) is a particularly noteworthy example of congressional delegation of rulemaking authority to federal agencies. A previous CRS report identified more than 40 provisions in PPACA that require or permit the issuance of rules to implement the legislation.

One way for Congress to identify upcoming PPACA rules is by reviewing the Unified Agenda of Federal Regulatory and Deregulatory Actions, which is published twice each year (spring and fall) by the Regulatory Information Service Center (RISC), a component of the U.S. General Services Administration, for the Office of Management and Budget's (OMB) Office of Information and Regulatory Affairs (OIRA). The Unified Agenda lists upcoming activities, by agency, in five separate categories or stages of the rulemaking process: the prerule stage, the proposed rule stage, the final rule stage, long-term actions, and completed actions. All entries in the Unified Agenda have uniform data elements,

---

* This is an edited, reformatted and augmented version of a Congressional Research Service publication, CRS Report for Congress R41963, from www.crs.gov, dated August 18, 2011.

including the department and agency issuing the rule, the title of the rule, its Regulation Identifier Number (RIN), an abstract describing the nature of action being taken, and a timetable showing the dates of past actions and a projected date for the next regulatory action. Each entry also contains an element indicating the priority of the regulation (e.g., whether it is considered "economically significant" under Executive Order 12866, or whether it is considered a "major" rule under the Congressional Review Act).

This report examines the most recent edition of the Unified Agenda, published on July 7, 2011 (the second edition that RISC compiled and issued after the enactment of PPACA). The report identifies upcoming proposed and final rules listed in the July 7, 2011, Unified Agenda that are expected to be issued pursuant to PPACA. The **Appendix** lists these upcoming proposed and final rules in a table. The report also briefly discusses the longterm actions listed in the Unified Agenda, as well as some options for congressional oversight over the PPACA rules.

INTRODUCTION

Federal regulations generally result from an act of Congress and are the means by which statutes are implemented and specific requirements are established. Congress delegates rulemaking authority to agencies for a variety of reasons and in a variety of ways. The Patient Protection and Affordable Care Act (PPACA; P.L. 111-148, as amended) is a particularly noteworthy example of congressional delegation of rulemaking authority to federal agencies.[1] PPACA is a comprehensive overhaul of the health care system that includes such provisions as the expansion of eligibility for Medicaid, amendments to Medicare that are intended to reduce its growth, an individual mandate for the purchase of health insurance, and the establishment of insurance exchanges through which individuals and families can receive federal subsidies to help them purchase insurance. A previous CRS report identified more than 40 provisions in PPACA that require or permit the issuance of rules to implement the legislation.[2]

The rules that agencies issue pursuant to PPACA are expected to have a major impact on how the legislation is implemented. For example, in an article entitled "The War Isn't Over" that was posted on the *New England Journal of Medicine's* Health Care Reform Center shortly after PPACA was signed into law, Henry J. Aaron and Robert D. Reischauer wrote:

> Making the legislation a success requires not only that it survive but also that it be effectively implemented. Although the bill runs to more than 2000 pages, much remains to be decided. The legislation tasks federal or state officials with writing regulations, making appointments, and giving precise meaning to many terms. Many of these actions will provoke controversy.... Far from having ended, the war to make health care reform an enduring success has just begun. Winning that war will require administrative determination and imagination and as much political resolve as was needed to pass the legislation.[3]

Mandatory and Discretionary Rulemaking Provisions

The manner in which Congress delegates rulemaking authority to federal agencies determines the amount of discretion the agencies have in crafting the rules and, conversely, the amount of control that Congress retains for itself. Some of the more than 40 rulemaking provisions in PPACA are quite specific, stipulating the substance of the rules, whether certain consultative or rulemaking procedures should be used, and deadlines for their issuance or implementation.[4] Other provisions in PPACA permit, but do not require, the agencies to issue certain rules (e.g., stating that the head of an agency "may issue regulations" defining certain terms, or "may by regulation" establish guidance or requirements for carrying out the legislation). As a result, the agency head has the discretion to decide whether to issue any regulations at all, and if so, what those rules will contain. Still other provisions in PPACA require agencies to establish programs or procedures but do not specifically mention regulations. By December 2010, federal agencies had already issued at least 18 final rules implementing sections of PPACA.[5] Although the legislation specifically required or permitted some of the rules to be published, other rules implemented PPACA provisions that did not specifically mention rulemaking. The use of rulemaking in these cases does not appear to be either improper or unusual; if the requirements in those rules were intended to be binding on the public, rulemaking may have been the agencies only viable option to implement the related statutory provisions.[6]

Congressional Oversight and the Unified Agenda

In his book *Building a Legislative-Centered Public Administration*, David H. Rosenbloom noted that rulemaking and lawmaking are functionally equivalent (the results of both processes have the force of law), and that when agencies issue rules they, in effect, legislate. He went on to say that the "Constitution's grant of legislative power to Congress encompasses a responsibility to ensure that delegated authority is exercised according to appropriate procedures."[7] Congressional oversight of rulemaking can deal with a variety of issues, including the substance of the rules issued pursuant to congressional delegations of authority and the process by which those rules are issued.

For Congress to oversee the regulations being issued to implement PPACA, it would help to have an early sense of what rules the agencies are going to issue, and when. The previously mentioned CRS report identifying the provisions in the act that require or permit rulemaking can be useful in this regard.[8] However, the legislation did not indicate when some of the mandatory rules should be issued, some of the rules that the agencies are permitted (but not required) to issue may never be developed, and many of the rules that the agencies have already issued to implement PPACA were not specifically mentioned in the act.

The Unified Agenda

A potentially better way for Congress to identify upcoming PPACA rules is by reviewing the Unified Agenda of Federal Regulatory and Deregulatory Actions (hereafter, Unified Agenda), which is published twice each year (usually in the spring and fall) by the Regulatory Information Service Center (RISC), a component of the U.S. General Services Administration, for the Office of Management and Budget's (OMB) Office of Information and Regulatory Affairs (OIRA).[9] The Unified Agenda helps agencies fulfill two current transparency requirements:

- The Regulatory Flexibility Act (5 U.S.C. § 602) requires that all agencies publish semiannual regulatory agendas in the *Federal Register* describing regulatory actions that they are developing that may have a significant economic impact on a substantial number of small entities.[10]
- Section 4 of Executive Order 12866 on "Regulatory Planning and Review" requires that all executive branch agencies "prepare an agenda of all regulations under development or review."[11] The stated purposes of this and other planning requirements in the order are, among other things, to "maximize consultation and the resolution of potential conflicts at an early stage" and to "involve the public and its

State, local, and tribal officials in regulatory planning." The executive order also requires that each agency prepare, as part of the fall edition of the Unified Agenda, a "regulatory plan" of the most important significant regulatory actions that the agency reasonably expects to issue in proposed or final form during the upcoming fiscal year.

The Unified Agenda lists upcoming activities, by agency, in five separate categories or stages of the rulemaking process:

- prerule stage (e.g., advance notices of proposed rulemaking that are expected to be issued in the next 12 months);
- proposed rule stage (i.e., notices of proposed rulemaking that are expected to be issued in the next 12 months, or for which the closing date of the comment period is the next step);
- final rule stage (i.e., final rules or other final actions that are expected to be issued in the next 12 months);
- long-term actions (i.e., items under development that agencies do not expect to take action on in the next 12 months); and
- completed actions (i.e., final rules or rules that have been withdrawn since the last edition of the Unified Agenda).

All entries in the Unified Agenda have uniform data elements, including the department and agency issuing the rule, the title of the rule, its Regulation Identifier Number (RIN),[12] an abstract describing the nature of action being taken, and a timetable showing the dates of past actions and a projected date (sometimes just the projected month and year) for the next regulatory action. Each entry also contains an element indicating the priority of the regulation (e.g., whether it is considered "economically significant" under Executive Order 12866, or whether it is considered a "major" rule under the Congressional Review Act).[13]

There is no penalty for issuing a rule without a prior notice in the Unified Agenda, and some prospective rules listed in the Unified Agenda never get issued, reflecting the fluid nature of the rulemaking process. Nevertheless, the Unified Agenda can help Congress and the public know what regulatory actions are about to occur, and it arguably provides federal agencies with the most systematic, government-wide method to alert the public about their upcoming proposed rules. A previously issued CRS report indicated that about three-fourths of the significant proposed rules published after having been reviewed by OIRA in 2008 were previously listed in the "proposed rule" section of the Unified Agenda.[14]

This Report

The July 7, 2011, edition of the Unified Agenda and Regulatory Plan is the second edition that RISC has compiled and issued after the enactment of PPACA.[15] Federal agencies were required to submit data to RISC for the Unified Agenda by February 25, 2011,[16] but some items were subsequently updated during the OIRA review process.[17]

This report examines the July 7, 2011, edition of the Unified Agenda and identifies upcoming proposed and final rules and long-term actions that were expected to be issued pursuant to PPACA in the next 12 months. To identify those upcoming rules and actions, CRS searched all fields of the Unified Agenda (all agencies) using the term "Affordable Care Act," focusing on the proposed rule and final rule stages of rulemaking, and also including the "long-term actions" category.

The results of the search for proposed and final rules are provided in the **Appendix** to this report. For each upcoming proposed and final rule listed, the table identifies the department and agency expected to issue the rule, the title of the rule and its RIN, an abstract describing the nature of the rulemaking action, and the date that the proposed or final rule was expected to be issued.[18] The abstracts presented in the table were taken verbatim from the Unified Agenda entries. Within the proposed and final rule sections of the table, the entries are organized by agency.

Because agencies were compiling the information early in the year, their estimates for when upcoming proposed and final rules would be issued may have been out of date by the time the Unified Agenda was published. To provide the most up-to-date information, on August 3, 2011, CRS electronically searched the *Federal Register* to see whether the proposed and final rules listed in the Unified Agenda had been published. This information is provided in the table. If the proposed or final rule was published as of August 3, the *Federal Register* citation is also provided.

The July 7, 2011, edition of the Unified Agenda listed 41 PPACA-related actions in the "proposed rule stage" (indicating that the agencies expected to issue proposed rules on the topics within the next 12 months, or for which the closing dates of the comment periods are the next step).

UPCOMING PPACA PROPOSED RULES

Thirty-three of the 41 upcoming proposed rules were expected to be issued by components of the Department of Health and Human Services (HHS): the Health Resources and Services Administration (HRSA, four actions); the Food and Drug Administration (FDA, two actions); Indian Health Service (IHS, two actions); the Centers for Medicare and Medicaid Policy (CMS, 21 actions); the Administration on Aging (AOA, one action); and the Office of the Secretary (OS, three actions). Other proposed rules were expected to be issued by the Department of Labor's (DOL) Employee Benefits Security Administration (EBSA, one action); the DOL's Office of Workers' Compensation Programs (OWCP, one action); the Treasury Department's Departmental Offices (DO, one action); the Internal Revenue Service (IRS, two actions); and the Office of Personnel Management (OPM, three actions).

Timing of the Proposed Rules

The agencies indicated that 17 of the 41 items in the "proposed rule" section of the Unified Agenda would be issued by the end of July 2011.[19] As of August 3, 2011, 9 of these 17 anticipated notices of proposed rulemaking (NPRMs) had been published, and 8 had not yet been published. Some of the rules for which NPRMs have been published include an HHS/HRSA rule on "340B Orphan Drug Exclusion;"[20]

- an HHS/FDA rule on "Food Labeling: Nutrition Labeling for Food Sold in Vending Machines;"[21]
- an HHS/CMS rule on "Availability of Medicare Data for Performance Measurement;"[22] and
- an HHS/CMS rule on "Establishment of the Consumer Operated and Oriented Plan Program."[23]

Some of the eight proposed rules that were expected to be published by the end of July 2011, but that had not been published as of August 3, 2011, include

- an HHS/HRSA rule on "Elimination of Duplication Between the Healthcare Integrity and Protection Data Bank and the National Practitioner Data Bank;"

- an HHS/CMS rule on "Administrative Simplification: Standard Unique Identifier for Health Plans;"
- an HHS/CMS rule on "Medicaid Eligibility Expansion Under the Affordable Care Act of 2010;" and
- a Treasury/IRS rule on "Development and Utilization of Uniform Explanation of Coverage Documents, Definitions, and Requirements To Provide Information Under the Patient Protection and Affordable Care Act."

Several other proposed rules were expected to be issued later in 2011, including

- an HHS/IHS rule on "Standards for the Planning, Design, Construction and Operation of Health Care and Sanitation Facilities" (expected to be published in December 2011);
- an HHS/CMS rule on "Implementing Regulations for Reauthorization of the Children's Health Insurance Program (CHIP)" (expected to be published in December 2011);
- an HHS/OS rule on "Nondiscrimination Under the Affordable Care Act" (expected to be published in September 2011); and
- an OPM rule on "Federal Employees Health Benefits Program; Disputed Claims and External Review Requirements" (expected to be published in September 2011).

Notable Proposed Rules

HHS agencies considered 4 of the 41 items in the "proposed rule" section of the Unified Agenda important enough to be included in the regulatory plan:

- Two HHS/FDA rules on "Food Labeling: Nutrition Labeling for Food Sold in Vending Machines," which the agency published as an NPRM on April 6, 2011;[24] and "Food Labeling: Nutrition Labeling of Standard Menu Items in Restaurants and Similar Retail Food Establishments," which the agency published as an NPRM on April 6, 2011;[25]
- An HHS/CMS rule on "Medicare Shared Savings Program: Accountable Care Organizations," which the agency published as an NPRM on April 7, 2011;[26] and

- An HHS/AOA rule on "Community Living Assistance Services and Supports (CLASS) Program—Designation of the CLASS Independence Benefit Plan and Enrollment Rules," which the agency expects to publish as an NPRM in October 2011.

Economically Significant or Major Proposed Rules

In addition to the PPACA-related "proposed rule" actions that were listed in the regulatory plan, the Unified Agenda listed eight other actions that the agencies considered "economically significant" or "major" (one definition of "economically significant" or "major," for example, is that the rule is expected to have at least a $100 million annual effect on the economy). Examples include

- an HHS/CMS rule on "Medicaid Eligibility Expansion Under the Affordable Care Act of 2010," which was expected to be published as an NPRM sometime during June 2011, but had not been published as of August 3, 2011;
- an HHS/CMS rule on "Requirements To Implement American Health Benefit Exchanges and Other Provisions of the Affordable Care Act," which was published as an NPRM on July 15, 2011;[27] and
- an HHS/OCIIO rule on "Public Use Files of Health Plan Data," which is expected to be issued sometime during December 2011.

"Other Significant" Proposed Rules

In addition to the above-mentioned rules, the agencies characterized 27 of the 41 actions that were listed in the "proposed rule" section of the Unified Agenda as "other significant," indicating that although they were not listed in the regulatory plan or expected to be "economically significant," they were expected to be significant enough to be reviewed by OIRA under Executive Order 12866.[28] These proposed rules included

- an HHS/IHS rule on "Confidentiality of Medical Quality Assurance Records; Qualified Immunity for Participants," which the agency expects to publish in February 2012;
- an HHS/CMS rule on "Face-to-Face Requirements for Home Health Services; Policy Changes and Clarifications Related to Home Health," which the agency published on July 12, 2011;[29]
- an HHS/AOA rule on "Community Living Assistance Services and Supports (CLASS) Program—Designation of the CLASS

Independence Benefit Plan and Enrollment Rules," which the agency expects to issue in October 2011; and

- a DOL/OWCP rule on "Regulations Implementing Amendments to the Black Lung Benefits Act: Determining Coal Miners and Survivors Entitlement to Benefits," which the agency expects to issue in March 2012.

Effects on Small Entities

The Regulatory Flexibility Act (5 U.S.C. §§ 601-612) generally requires federal agencies to assess the impact of their forthcoming regulations on "small entities" (i.e., small businesses, small governments, and small not-for-profit organizations).[30] Three of the previously-mentioned PPACA-related rules listed in the "proposed rule" section were expected to affect small businesses, small governments, or both, and were expected to require a regulatory flexibility analysis:

- Two HHS/FDA rules on "Food Labeling: Nutrition Labeling for Food Sold in Vending Machines," and "Food Labeling: Nutrition Labeling of Standard Menu Items in Chain Restaurants;" and
- An HHS/CMS rule on "Medicaid Eligibility Expansion Under the Affordable Care Act of 2010."

In addition to these rules, eight other actions listed in the "proposed rule" section were expected to have an effect on small businesses, small governments, or small not-for-profits, but the agencies either did not expect to the rules to trigger the requirements of the Regulatory Flexibility Act, or were undecided as to whether they would do so. These actions included

- an HHS/CMS rule on "Administrative Simplification: Standard Unique Identifier for Health Plans;"
- an HHS/CMS rule on "Durable Medical Equipment (DME) Face to Face Encounters and Written Orders Prior to Delivery;" and
- a DOL/EBSA rule on "Ex Parte Cease and Desist and Summary Seizure Orders Under ERISA Section 521."

The July 7, 2011, edition of the Unified Agenda listed 13 PPACA-related actions in the "final rule stage" section (indicating that the agencies expected to issue final rules on the subjects within the next 12 months).

Upcoming PPACA Final Rules

Eight of the upcoming final rules were expected to be issued by CMS; two by the IRS; and one each by HRSA, the Occupational Safety and Health Administration (OSHA) within DOL, and the Social Security Administration.

Timing of Final Rules

The agencies indicated that 6 of the 13 items in the "final rule" section of the Unified Agenda would be issued by the end of July 2011. As of August 3, 2011, four of these rules had been issued:

- An HHS/CMS rule on "Administrative Simplification: Adoption of Authoring Organizations for Operating Rules and Adoption of Operating Rules for Eligibility and Claims Status;" which was published as an interim final rule on July 8, 2011; [31]
- An HHS/CMS rule on "Payment Adjustment for Provider—Preventable Conditions Including Health Care-Acquired Conditions," which was published as a final rule on June 6, 2011;[32]
- An HHS/CMS rule on "Enhanced Federal Funding for Medicaid Eligibility Determination and Enrollment Activities," which was published as a final rule on April 19, 2011; [33] and
- An HHS/CMS rule on "Internal Claims, Appeals, and External Review Processes Under the Affordable Care Act," which was originally published as an interim final rule on July 23, 2010, followed by a second interim final rule on June 24, 2011. [34]

As of August 3, 2011, the remaining two final rules that the agencies indicated would be published by the end of July 2011 had not been published:

- An HHS/CMS rule on "Changes to the Demonstration Review and Approval Process," and
- An IRS rule on "Development and Utilization of Uniform Explanation of Coverage Documents, Definitions, and Requirements To Provide Information Under the Patient Protection and Affordable Care Act."

The agencies indicated that six other final rules would be published sometime in 2011:

- An HHS/HRSA rule on "Designation of Medically Underserved Populations and Health Professional Shortage Areas," which was expected to be issued in November 2011;
- An HHS/CMS rule on "Administrative Simplification: Adoption of Standard and Operating Rule for Electronic Funds Transfer (EFT) and Operating Rule for Remittance Advice," which was expected to be issued in December 2011;
- An HHS/CMS rule on "Medicaid Recovery Audit Contractors," which was expected to be issued in August 2011;
- An HHS/CMS rule on "Community First Choice Option," which was expected to be issued in August 2011;
- A DOL/OSHA rule on "Procedures for the Handling of Retaliation Complaints Under Section 1558 of the Affordable Care Act," which was expected to be issued in September 2011; and
- An IRS rule on "Indoor Tanning Services," which was expected to be issued in December 2011.

Notable Final Rules

None of the rules that were listed in the "final rule" section of the Unified Agenda were considered important enough to be included in the agencies' regulatory plans.

Economically Significant or Major Final Rules

The Unified Agenda listed three entries in the "final rule" section that were considered "economically significant" or "major" (e.g., that were expected to have at least a $100 million annual effect on the economy). All three rules were CMS rules: (1) "Medicaid Recovery Audit Contractors;" (2) "Community First Choice Option;" and (3) "Enhanced Federal Funding for Medicaid Eligibility Determination and Enrollment Activities."

"Other Significant" Final Rules

In addition to the above-mentioned rules, eight other entries in the "final rule" section of the Unified Agenda were characterized as "other significant," indicating that although they were not listed in the regulatory plan or expected to be "economically significant," they were expected to be significant enough to be reviewed by OIRA under Executive Order 12866. These final rules included:

- an HHS/HRSA rule on "Designation of Medically Underserved Populations and Health Professional Shortage Areas;"
- an HHS/CMS rule on "Administrative Simplification: Adoption of Standard and Operating Rule for Electronic Funds Transfer (EFT) and Operating Rule for Remittance Advice;"
- a DOL/OSHA rule on "Procedures for the Handling of Retaliation Complaints Under Section 1558 of the Affordable Care Act of 2010;" and
- a Social Security Administration rule on "Regulations Regarding Income-Related Monthly Adjustment Amounts to Medicare Beneficiaries' Prescription Drug Premiums."

Effects on Small Entities

Two of the upcoming final rules were expected to trigger the requirements of the Regulatory Flexibility Act because of their effects on small businesses: the CMS rule on "Enhanced Federal Funding for Medicaid Eligibility Determination and Enrollment Activities," and the IRS rule on "Indoor Tanning Services."

Three other CMS rules were expected to have an effect on small businesses, governments, or other organizations, but were not expected to require a regulatory flexibility analysis: (1) "Administrative Simplification: Adoption of Standard and Operating Rule for Electronic Funds Transfer (EFT) and Operating Rule for Remittance Advice;" (2) "Administrative Simplification: Adoption of Authoring Organizations for Operating Rules and Adoption of Operating Rules for Eligibility and Claims Status;" and (3) "Medicaid Recovery Audit Contractors."

PPACA Long-Term Actions

As noted earlier in this report, the Unified Agenda also identifies "long-term actions"—that is, regulatory actions that are under development in the agencies that the agencies do not expect to take action on in the next 12 months. The July 7, 2011 edition of the Unified Agenda listed 27 long-term actions related to PPACA. In comparison with the proposed and final rules previously discussed, it is much less clear when the PPACA-related long-term actions are expected to occur; in 17 of the 27 cases, the agencies said that the dates for the actions were "to be determined." Of the remaining ten long-term actions, six were expected in June 2012, one in August 2012, one in calendar year 2013, and two in calendar year 2014.

Nature of the Long-Term Actions

Of the 27 long-term actions, 15 were upcoming final rules that were expected to be issued once the agency had considered the comments received in response to previously issued interim final rules.[35] These actions included

- an HHS/CMS rule on "Requirements for Long-Term Care Facilities: Notification of Facility Closure;" with the final rule expected to be published in February 2014;"[36] and
- a DOL/EBSA rule on "Preexisting Condition Exclusions, Lifetime and Annual Limits, Rescissions and Patient Protections Under the Affordable Care Act," with the date of the final rule "to be determined."[37]

The eight other long-term actions were upcoming final rules that the agency expected to issue after considering the comments received in response to a previously issued notice of proposed rulemaking. These actions included

- an HHS/CMS rule on "Affordable Care Act Waiver for State Innovation; Review and Approval Process;"[38] and
- an IRS rule on "Requirements Applicable to Group Health Plans and Health Insurance Issuers Under the Patient Protection and Affordable Care Act, I."[39]

The four other PPACA-related long-term actions included

- an HHS/CMS NPRM on "Long-Term Care Facility Quality Assessment and Performance Improvement Dementia Management and Abuse Prevention Training," and
- a DOL/EBSA unspecified rulemaking action on "Automatic Enrollment in Health Plans of Employees of Large Employers Under FLSA Section 18A ;"

Notable Long-Term Actions

The agencies identified 10 of the 27 PPACA-related long-term actions as "economically significant," "major," or both. Nine of these actions were cases in which the agencies had issued interim final rules and were reviewing the comments received. These included

- two HHS/CMS actions on such topics as "Preexisting Condition Exclusions, Lifetime and Annual Limits, Prohibition on Discrimination and Patient Protections;" "Preventive Services Under the Affordable Care Act;" "Affordable Care Act Waiver for State Innovation; Review and Approval Process;" and
- a DOL/EBSA action entitled "Group Health Plans and Health Insurance Coverage Relating to Status as a Grandfathered Health Plan Under the Patient Protection and Affordable Care Act."

One other long-term action that was identified as major was a CMS rule on "Affordable Care Act Waiver for State Innovation; Review and Approval Process." The agency published an NPRM on March 14 and will be taking final action at a later date "to be determined."

The agencies considered 12 of the 27 actions to be "other significant," meaning that the agencies considered them significant enough to be reviewed by OIRA under Executive Order 12866, but not "economically significant." These actions included

- an HHS/IHS rule on "Catastrophic Health Emergency Fund (CHEF);"
- two HHS/CMS actions entitled "Health Care Reform Insurance Web Portal Requirements" and "Student Health Insurance Coverage;" and
- a DOL/EBSA action on "Automatic Enrollment in Health Plans of Employees of Large Employers Under FLSA Section 18A."

Congressional Oversight Options

As noted earlier in this report, when federal agencies issue substantive regulations, they are carrying out legislative authority delegated to them by Congress. Therefore, it is appropriate for Congress to oversee the rules that agencies issue to ensure that they are consistent with congressional intent and the rulemaking requirements established in various statutes and executive orders. For Congress to oversee the rules being issued pursuant to PPACA, it must first know that they are being issued—ideally as early as possible. The Unified Agenda is perhaps the best vehicle to provide that early information, describing not only what rules are expected to be issued, but also providing information regarding their significance and timing.

Congress has a range of tools available to oversee the rules that federal agencies are expected to issue to implement PPACA, including oversight hearings and confirmation hearings for the heads of regulatory agencies. Individual Members of Congress may also participate in the rulemaking process by, among other things, meeting with agency officials and filing public comments.[40] Congress, committees, and individual Members can also request that the Government Accountability Office (GAO) evaluate the agencies' rulemaking activities.

Another option is the Congressional Review Act (CRA; 5 U.S.C. §§801-808), which was enacted in 1996 to establish procedures detailing congressional authority over rulemaking "without at the same time requiring Congress to become a super regulatory agency."[41] The act generally requires federal agencies to submit all of their covered final rules to both houses of Congress and GAO before they can take effect.[42] It also established expedited legislative procedures (primarily in the Senate) by which Congress may disapprove agencies' final rules by enacting a joint resolution of disapproval.[43] The definition of a covered rule in the CRA is quite broad, arguably including any type of document (e.g., legislative rules, policy statements, guidance, manuals, and memoranda) that the agency wishes to make binding on the affected public.[44] After these rules are submitted, Congress can use the expedited procedures specified in the CRA to disapprove any of the rules. CRA resolutions of disapproval must be presented to the President for signature or veto.

For a variety of reasons, however, the CRA has been used to disapprove only one rule in the 14 years since it was enacted.[45] Perhaps most notably, it is likely that a President would veto a resolution of disapproval to protect rules developed under his own administration, and it may be difficult for Congress to muster the two-thirds vote in both houses needed to overturn the veto. Congress can also use regular (i.e., non-CRA) legislative procedures to disapprove agencies' rules, but such legislation may prove even more difficult to enact than a CRA resolution of disapproval (primarily because of the lack of expedited procedures in the Senate), and if enacted may also be vetoed by the President.

Appendix. Upcoming Proposed and Final Rules Pursuant to the Patient Protection and Affordable Care Act

Department/Agency	Title of Rule (RIN)	Abstract, as Provided in the Unified Agenda	Expected Publication Date
Proposed Rules			
HHS/HRSA	Elimination of Duplication Between the Healthcare Integrity and Protection Data Bank and the National Practitioner Data Bank (0906-AA87)	This rule is required under the Affordable Care Act. The purpose is to eliminate the redundant reporting requirements for two closely related national health care data banks. This rule terminates the Healthcare Integrity and Protection Databank (HIPDB) and transfers all data collected in the HIPDB to the National Practitioner Data Bank (NPDB) established pursuant to the Health Care Quality Improvement Act of 1986. This rule will also provide for the disclosure of information, fee collection, establishment of dispute procedures, and an effective date of no later than one year after enactment or when regulations are published.	07/2011 Note: Although the Agenda indicates that there is a statutory deadline for this rule, it does not specify what the deadline is. No NPRM had been published as of 08/03/2011.
HHS/HRSA	340B Drug Pricing Program; Manufacturer Civil Monetary Penalties (0906-AA89)	This rulemaking is required under the Affordable Care Act. The purpose is to implement an enhancement to the 340B Program. It amends section 340B of the Public Health Service Act to impose monetary sanctions (not to exceed $5,000 per instance) on drug manufacturers who intentionally charge a covered entity (aka "safety net provider") a price above the ceiling price established under the procedures of the 340B Program.	07/2011 Note: An advance notice of proposed rulemaking (ANPRM) was published on 09/20/2010 (75 F.R. 57230). Legal deadline for ANPRM was 09/20/2010. No NPRM had been published as of 08/03/2011.
HHS/HRSA	340B Ceiling Price Regulations (0906-AA92)	The purpose of this rulemaking is to implement a new statutory requirement in the Affordable Care Act to develop and publish through an appropriate policy or regulation issuance, precisely defined standards and methodology for the calculation of ceiling prices for purposes of 340B.	11/2011

Department/Agency	Title of Rule (RIN)	Abstract, as Provided in the Unified Agenda	Expected Publication Date
HHS/HRSA	340B Orphan Drug Exclusion (0906-AA94)	Under the changes made by section 2302 Health Care and Education Reconciliation Act (P.L. 111-152), orphan drugs, when used for the rare condition or disease for which that orphan drug was designated under section 526 of the Federal Food, Drug, and Cosmetic Act (FFDCA), are excluded from the definition of covered outpatient drug for the specified newly-eligible covered entity types for purposes of the 340B [Drug Pricing] Program. This regulatory action details how these exclusions will be implemented under the 340B [Drug Pricing] Program. The purpose of issuing this proposed rule is to clarify HHS's stated effort in: (1) Providing clarity in the marketplace, (2) maintaining the 340B savings and interests to the newly-eligible covered entities; and (3) protecting the financial incentives for manufacturing orphan drugs designated for a rare disease or condition as indicated in the Affordable Care Act as intended by Congress.	05/20/2011 Note: NPRM was published on 05/20/2011 (76 F.R. 29183).
HHS/FDA	Food Labeling: Nutrition Labeling for Food Sold in Vending Machines (0910-AG56)	The Food and Drug Administration (FDA) is proposing regulations to establish requirements for nutrition labeling of certain food sold in certain vending machines. FDA is also proposing the terms and conditions for vending machine operators registering to voluntarily be subject to the requirements of section 4205. FDA is taking this action to carry out section 4205 of the Patient Protection and Affordable Care Act ("Affordable Care Act" or "ACA"), which was signed into law on March 23, 2010.	04/06/2011 Note: NPRM was published on 04/06/2011 (76 F.R. 19238). Legal deadline for the proposed rule was 03/23/2010.

Appendix. (Continued)

Department/Agency	Title of Rule (RIN)	Abstract, as Provided in the Unified Agenda	Expected Publication Date
HHS/FDA	Food Labeling: Nutrition Labeling of Standard Menu Items in Restaurants and Similar Retail Food Establishments (0910-AG57)	The Food and Drug Administration (FDA) is proposing regulations to establish requirements for nutrition labeling of standard menu items in chain restaurants and similar retail food establishments. FDA is also proposing the terms and conditions for restaurants and similar retail food establishments registering to voluntarily be subject to the requirements of section 4205. FDA is taking this action to carry out section 4205 of the Patient Protection and Affordable Care Act ("Affordable Care Act" or "ACA"), which was signed into law on March 23, 2010.	04/06/2011 Note: NPRM was published on 04/06/2011 (76 F.R. 19192). Legal deadline for the proposed rule was 03/23/2011.
HHS/IHS	Standards for the Planning, Design, Construction and Operation of Health Care and Sanitation Facilities (0917-AA08)	Section 311(c)(1) of the Indian Health Care Improvement Act, P.L. 94-437 (1976), as amended by the Patient Protection and Affordable Care Act, P.L. 111-148, section 10221 (2010) requires the Secretary, acting though the Indian Health Service (IHS), to establish, by regulation, standards for the planning, design, construction, and operation of health care and sanitation facilities serving Indians under the Indian Health Care Improvement Act. Additionally, these regulations would stipulate which departmental regulations would be applicable to these activities.	12/2011
HHS/IHS	Confidentiality of Medical Quality Assurance Records; Qualified Immunity for Participants (0917-AA09)	Section 805(j)) of the Indian Health Care Improvement Act, P.L. 94-437 (1976), as amended by the Patient Protection and Affordable Care Act, P.L. 111-148, section 10221 (2010) requires the Secretary of the Department of Health and Human Services, acting through the Indian Health Service (IHS), to promulgate regulations to implement section 805.	02/2012

Department/Agency	Title of Rule (RIN)	Abstract, as Provided in the Unified Agenda	Expected Publication Date
		Section 805 makes confidential and privileged the medical quality assurance records of Indian health programs and urban Indian organizations, with very limited exceptions. It also prohibits the testimony of individuals that review or create medical quality assurance records, with very limited exceptions. Although section 805 is immediately executable, the Secretary is required to issue regulations which could substantively affect the implementation of this provision.	
HHS/CMS	Home and Community-Based Services (HCBS) State Plan Services Program and 5-Year Approvals and Renewals for Waivers and Demonstration Projects(CMS-2249-P2) (0938-AO53)	In 2008, CMS issued a proposed rule that would define and describe State plan home and community-based services (HCBS) under the Deficit Reduction Act. This rule would allow States, at their option, to provide home and community-based services (HCBS) under their regular State Medicaid plans. This proposed rule revises the 2008 proposed rule to implement provisions of the Affordable Care Act that require oversight and assessment of the administration of home and community based services. In addition, this rule would respond to public comments received on the previous proposed rule pertaining to the HCBS benefit under the Medicaid State plan. Finally, this proposed rule would clarify that Medicaid waivers that provide services for individuals dually eligible for Medicare and Medicaid could be authorized for as long as 5 years. Any waiver that provides medical assistance for dual eligible individuals (including any waivers under which non-dual eligible individuals may be enrolled) may be conducted for a period of 5 years and, upon request by the State, may be extended for additional 5-year periods.	09/2011 (second NPRM) Note: Original NPRM was published on 04/04/2008 (73 F.R. 18676). HHS is revising that earlier NPRM in light of the Affordable Care Act.

Appendix. (Continued)

Department/Agency	Title of Rule (RIN)	Abstract, as Provided in the Unified Agenda	Expected Publication Date
HHS/CMS	Establishing Additional Medicare Provider and Supplier Enrollment Safeguards and Surety Bonds for DMEPOS (CMS-6045-P) (0938-AP01)	This proposed rule would expand existing provider and supplier enrollment requirements to obtain or maintain Medicare billing privileges. Under the Affordable Care Act, this rule would also require surety bonds for DMEPOS [Durable Medical Equipment, Prosthetics, Orthotics, and Supplies]. This proposed rule would also specify the qualification standards and the type of prosthetic and orthotic devices billable to the Medicare program. It also proposes the accreditation deadline for the entities billing orthotics and prosthetics and identifies the DMEPOS product categories exempt from accreditation requirements.	04/2012
HHS/CMS	Implementing Regulations for Reauthorization of the Children's Health Insurance Program (CHIP) (CMS-2301-P) (0938-AP68)	This proposed rule would introduce several new features as a result of the passage of the Children's Health Insurance Program Reauthorization Act (CHIPRA) including a CHIP performance bonus payment system through 2013. For example, the rule would define and provide more guidance on the parameters of the new Express Lane Eligibility option for States including what it means to be an Express Lane agency. It would also define the parameters for the new state option to cover pregnant women in CHIP and provide further guidance regarding the newly required dental benefit package. In addition, it would codify the definition of individuals who are lawfully residing in the US but who are not citizens who can be enrolled in Medicaid and CHIP. Under section 2102 of the Affordable Care Act, this rule would also make technical corrections to selected provisions in CHIPRA and the American Recovery and Reinvestment Act of 2009 (ARRA).	09/2011

Department/Agency	Title of Rule (RIN)	Abstract, as Provided in the Unified Agenda	Expected Publication Date
HHS/CMS	Administrative Simplification: Standard Unique Identifier for Health Plans (CMS-0040-P) (0938-AQ13)	This rule would implement provisions of the Affordable Care Act of 2010 under Administrative Simplification that establish a unique health plan identifier. This health plan identifier will be used to identify health plans in HIPAA [Health Insurance Portability and Accountability Act of 1996] standard transactions.	07/2011 Note: Legal deadline for the final rule is 10/01/2012. No NPRM had been published as of 08/03/2011.
HHS/CMS	Availability of Medicare Data for Performance Measurement (CMS-5059-P) (0938-AQ17)	Under the Affordable Care Act of 2010, this rule would authorize the release and use of standardized extracts of Medicare claims data to measure the performance of providers and suppliers in ways that protect patient privacy and in accordance with other requirements.	06/2011 Note: Legal deadline for the final rule is 01/01/2012. NPR was published on 06/08/2011 (76 F.R. 33566).
HHS/CMS	Durable Medical Equipment (DME) Face to Face Encounters and Written Orders Prior to Delivery (CMS-6033-P) (0938-AQ21)	This proposed rule would implement section 1834(a)(11)(B) of the Social Security Act, which was recently amended by the Affordable Care Act. We propose establishing a face-to-face encounter as a condition of payment for certain durable medical equipment (DME) items. When this face-to-face encounter is performed by a physician assistant, a nurse practitioner or a clinical nurse specialist, a physician must document that the face-to-face has occurred pursuant to the order being written. The complete list of covered items of DME that require a face-to-face encounter will be published annually in the Federal Register.	08/2011 Note: Legal deadline for the final rule is 01/01/2012. No NPRM had been published as of 08/03/2011.
HHS/CMS	Medicare Shared Savings Program: Accountable Care Organizations (CMS-1345-P) (0938-AQ22)	This proposed rule would implement Section 3022 of the ACA provisions relating to Medicare payments to providers of services and suppliers participating in Accountable Care Organizations (ACOs). Under these provisions, providers of services and suppliers can continue to receive traditional Medicare fee-for-service payments under Parts A and B, and be eligible for additional payments based on meeting specified quality and savings requirements.	04/07/2011 Note: NRPM was published on 04/07/2011 (76 F.R. 19528). Final action is expected 01/2012. Legal deadline for the final rule is 01/01/2012.

Appendix. (Continued)

Department/Agency	Title of Rule (RIN)	Abstract, as Provided in the Unified Agenda	Expected Publication Date
HHS/CMS	Medicaid and Children's Health Insurance Programs; Disallowance of Claims for FFP and Technical Corrections (CMS-2292-P) (0938-AQ32)	This proposed rule would provide policy guidance to States requesting a reconsideration of a disallowance of Medicaid claims under the Medicare Improvements for Patients and Providers Act (MIPPA). Also, this rule would address provisions of the Affordable Care Act concerning the reconsideration process, the change from 60 days to 1-year for overpayments, and changes to the disallowance repayment schedule.	07/2011 Note: Legal deadline for the final rule was 03/23/2010. NPR was published on 08/03/2011 (76 F.R. 46684).
HHS/CMS	Face-to-Face Requirements for Home Health Services; Policy Changes and Clarifications Related to Home Health (CMS-2348-P) (0938-AQ36)	This proposed rule under the Affordable Care Act of 2010 would require a physician to have a face-to-face encounter with an individual prior to issuing a certification for home health services.	08/2011 Note: Legal deadline for the final rule was 01/01/2010. NPR was published on 07/12/2011 (76 F.R. 41032).
HHS/CMS	Covered Outpatient Drugs (CMS-2345-P) (0938-AQ41)	This proposed rule would implement several provisions of the Affordable Care Act of 2010 that pertain to prescription drugs under the Medicaid program. It would revise the rebate formulas for covered outpatient drugs, revise the definition of average manufacturer price, and revise the Federal Upper Limits for multiple source drugs.	06/2011 Note: Legal deadline for the final rule was 01/01/2010. No NPRM had been published as of 08/03/2011.

Department/Agency	Title of Rule (RIN)	Abstract, as Provided in the Unified Agenda	Expected Publication Date
HHS/CMS	Medicaid Automated Data System Requirements and Data Elements Necessary for Program Integrity, Program Oversight, and Administration (CMS-2317-P) (0938-AQ43)	This proposed rule would implement several provisions of the Affordable Care Act of 2010. It would implement the provision that requires States, for data submitted on or after January 1, 2010, to include data elements from the automated data system that CMS determines to be necessary for program integrity, program oversight, and administration, at such frequency as CMS shall determine. It also would implement the provision that requires for managed care patients that the managed care plans provide data to States at a frequency and level of detail as specified by CMS. In addition, the rule would implement the provision that provides for withholding of Federal Matching Payments to States that fail to report enrollee encounter data in the Medicaid Statistical Information System.	10/2011 Note: Legal deadline for the final rule is 01/01/2010.
HHS/CMS	Compliance Program For Providers and Suppliers (CMS-6037-P) (0938-AQ58)	This proposed rule implements several provisions of the Affordable Care Act. Section 6401 requires the Secretary to establish the core elements of a compliance program for Medicare, Medicaid and SCHIP providers and suppliers. The compliance program would now be a condition of enrollment. Section 6402(c) requires the Secretary to establish appropriate administrative remedies for any beneficiary that knowingly participated in fraud. Finally, section 6402(d) requires that the Secretary to establish a process for a provider or supplier to return an overpayment to the program, as well establish a process for CMS and its contractors to receive and apply the overpayment.	11/2011

Appendix. (Continued)

Department/Agency	Title of Rule (RIN)	Abstract, as Provided in the Unified Agenda	Expected Publication Date
HHS/CMS	Federal Medicaid Assistance Percentages—Methodologies for Calculation of Enhanced Rate (CMS-2327-P) (0938-AQ59)	The Affordable Care Act authorizes enhanced Federal Medical Assistance Percentages (FMAP) for newly eligible individuals as defined by the act. This proposed rule sets forth methodologies for FMAP calculations.	06/2011 Note: Legal deadline for the final rule is 01/01/2014. No NPRM had been published as of 08/03/2011.
HHS/CMS	Medicaid Eligibility Expansion Under the Affordable Care Act of 2010 (CMS-2349-P) (0938-AQ62)	The Affordable Care Act authorizes a major Medicaid expansion to individuals who are under 65, not pregnant, not receiving Medicare and not eligible for other mandatory eligibility categories. This proposed rule would set forth policies for Medicaid expansion including household income and household composition, coordination with Exchanges, simplifying and streamlining Medicaid eligibility determinations.	06/2011 Note: Legal deadline for the final rule is 01/01/2014. No NPRM had been published as of 08/03/2011.
HHS/CMS	Enrollment Requirement to Disclose Affiliation With Suspended, Revoked, or Excluded Providers (CMS-6038-P) (0938-AQ64)	This regulation would implement sections of the Affordable Care Act that require providers or suppliers seeking to enroll in Medicare, Medicaid, or CHIP to disclose any current or previous, direct or indirect affiliation with a provider that has uncollected debt, is subject to a payment suspension under a Federal health care program, has been excluded from Medicare, Medicaid or CHIP or has had its billing privileges denied or revoked. The Secretary may deny enrollment if it has been determined that a previous affiliation poses an undue risk of fraud to the program.	08/2011 Note: No NPRM had been publishe as of 08/03/2011.

Department/Agency	Title of Rule (RIN)	Abstract, as Provided in the Unified Agenda	Expected Publication Date
HHS/CMS	Requirements To Implement American Health Benefit Exchanges and Other Provisions of the Affordable Care Act (CMS-9989-P) (0938-AQ67)	The Affordable Care Act requires the establishment of health insurance exchanges –new, competitive, consumer-centered health insurance marketplaces – that will put greater control and greater choice in the hands of individuals and small businesses. The exchanges will make purchasing health insurance easier by providing eligible consumers and businesses with "one-stop-shopping" where they can compare and purchase health insurance coverage. The Affordable Care Act authorized grants to the states to help them design and establish exchanges in time for millions of Americans to choose their coverage for 2014. This proposed rule would establish the requirements for exchanges.	06/2011 Note: NPRM was published on 07/15/2011 (76 F.R. 41866).
HHS/CMS	Public Use Files of Health Plan Data (CMS-9984-P) (0938-AQ69)	The Affordable Care Act requires generating public use files on data that HHS collects from health plans, and includes specific data and their application (or not) to the Trade Secrets Act. This rule would clarify statutory requirements under the Affordable Care Act.	12/2011
HHS/CMS	Transparency Reporting (CMS-9985-P) (0938-AQ72)	The Affordable Care Act requires group health plans and health insurance issuers to submit specific information to the Secretary, the State insurance commissioner, and to make the information available to the public. This includes information on claims payment policies, the number of claims denied, data on rating practices and other information as determined by the Secretary. The provision also requires plans and issuers to provide to individuals upon request the amount of cost sharing that the individual would be responsible for paying for a specific item or service provided by a participating provider. This interim final rule would implement information disclosure provisions in section 2715A of the Public Health Service Act [PHSA], as added by the Affordable Care Act.	09/2011

Appendix. (Continued)

Department/Agency	Title of Rule (RIN)	Abstract, as Provided in the Unified Agenda	Expected Publication Date
HHS/CMS	Uniform Explanation of Benefits, Coverage Facts, and Standardized Definitions (CMS-9982-P) (0938-AQ73)	The Affordable Care Act requires the Secretary to develop standards for use by group health plans and health insurance issuers in compiling and providing a summary of benefits and coverage explanation that accurately describes benefits and coverage. The Secretary must also set standards for the definitions of terms used in health insurance coverage, including specific terms set out in the statute. Plans and issuers must provide information according to these standards no later than 24 months after enactment. This proposed rule would implement the information disclosure provisions in section 2715 of PHSA , as added by the Affordable Care Act.	06/2011 Note: Legal deadline for the final rule was 03/23/2011. No NPRM had been published as of 08/03/2011.
HHS/CMS	Administrative Simplification: Compliance: Health Plan Certification (CMS-0037-P) (0938-AQ85)	This rule proposes to implement provisions of the Affordable Care Act of 2010 under Administrative Simplification to certify that data and information systems are in compliance with any applicable standards and associated operating rules for electronic funds transfers, eligibility for a health plan, health claim status, and health care payment and remittance advice.	02/2012 Note: According to the Unified Agenda, the first phase of compliance deadline is December 31, 2013; second phase of compliance deadline is December 31, 2015.
HHS/CMS	Establishment of the Consumer Operated and Oriented Plan Program (CMS-9983-P) (0938-AQ98)	Under section 1322 of the Affordable Care Act, a Consumer Operated and Oriented Plan program (CO-OP program) must be established to foster the creation of "qualified nonprofit health insurance issuers" that will offer qualified health plans in the individual and small group markets. Such qualified nonprofit issuers must operate with a strong consumer focus and use any profits to lower premiums, improve benefits, or improve the quality of health care delivered to plan members.	06/2011 Note: Grants and loans must be awarded by 7/1/2013. NPRM was published on 07/20/2011 (76 F.R. 43237).

Department/Agency	Title of Rule (RIN)	Abstract, as Provided in the Unified Agenda	Expected Publication Date
HHS/AOA	Community Living Assistance Services and Supports (CLASS) Program— Designation of the CLASS Independence Benefit Plan and Enrollment Rules (0985-AA07)	The Department of Health and Human Services will issue rules to implement the Community Living Assistance Services and Supports (CLASS) program, which was enacted as part of the Affordable Care Act. Specifically, the rules will designate the CLASS Independence Benefit Plan and establish enrollment rules for the program. Participation in the program is voluntary.	10/2011 Note: Legal deadline for the final rule is 10/01/2012.
HHS/OS	Nondiscrimination Under the Affordable Care Act (0991-AB75)	The Department of Health and Human Services, Office for Civil Rights, will issue rules for covered entities with respect to prohibitions against discrimination on the basis of race, color, national origin, sex, age, and disability, as provided in Section 1557 of the Affordable Care Act. Section 1557 provides certain protections from discrimination by recipients of federal financial assistance, federally conducted programs, and entities established under Title I of the Affordable Care Act. This section also identifies additional forms of federal financial assistance to which the section will apply.	09/2011
HHS/OS	Oversight and Assessment of the Administration of Home and Community Based Services (0991-AB79)	Section 2402 (a) of the Patient Protection and Affordable Care Act requires the Secretary of Health and Human Services to develop regulations to ensure that home and community based service systems are designed to allocate resources for services in a manner that is responsive to the changing needs and choices of beneficiaries receiving home and community based services.	10/2011 Note: Final action expected in 09/2012.
HHS/OS	Medicare and State Health Care Programs: Fraud and Abuse; Revisions to the Office of Inspector General's Safe Harbors Under the	This rule would: 1) Safe Harbor Provisions: Add safe harbors under the anti-kickback statute addressing arrangements in the following areas (subject to certain conditions):	11/2011 Note: Legal deadline for NPRM is 11/2011.

Appendix. (Continued)

Department/Agency	Title of Rule (RIN)	Abstract, as Provided in the Unified Agenda	Expected Publication Date
	Antikickback Status, Exclusion Authorities, and Civil Monetary Penalty (0991-AB81)	waivers of Federal health care program beneficiary cost-sharing amounts in the context of certain government sponsored clinical trials and in the context of certain emergency medical services furnished by suppliers owned or operated by States or municipalities; certain local transportation provided to Federal health care program beneficiaries; certain waived or reduced cost-sharing amounts under Medicare Part D (codifying in regulations section 101(e) of the Medicare Prescription Drug Improvement and Modernization Act of 2003); and certain discounts in the price of "applicable drugs" of manufacturers furnished to "applicable beneficiaries" under the Medicare Coverage Gap Discount Program (pursuant to section 3301 of the [ACA]). In addition, this rule would re-propose expanding the existing safe harbor for certain waivers of beneficiary co-insurance and deductible amounts for Part A or Part B services for Medicare SELECT policyholders in accordance with an agreement between the Medicare SELECT issuer and a provider or supplier, in certain contexts. 2) OIG's Authority To Impose Civil Money Penalties and Assessments (610 Review): Revise 42 CFR part 1003, addressing the Office of Inspector General's authority to propose the imposition of civil money penalties and assessments by reorganizing and simplifying existing regulatory text and eliminating obsolete references contained in the current regulations.	

Department/Agency	Title of Rule (RIN)	Abstract, as Provided in the Unified Agenda	Expected Publication Date
		Among the proposed revisions, this rule would establish separate subparts within part 1003 for various categories of violations; clarify the availability of exclusion for certain violations in addition to civil money penalties and assessments; date various references to managed care organization authorities; and clarify the application of section 1140 of the [SSA] with respect to the misuse of certain Departmental symbols, emblems, or names through Internet and e mail communications. 3) OIG's Exclusion Authority: In accordance with section 949 of the Medicare Prescription Drug Improvement and Modernization Act of 2003, and section 6402 of the [ACA], this rule would revise the OIG's exclusion authority to permit any Federal health care program to request a waiver of an OIG exclusion imposed under sections 1128(a)(1), 1128(a)(3), or 1128(a)(4) of the [SSA] if the exclusion would impose a hardship on beneficiaries. In addition, in accordance with sections 6406 and 6408 of the [ACA], the proposed rule would revise the OIG's exclusion authority to grant testimonial subpoena authority in exclusion cases; to add a new permissive exclusion authority for making false statements or misrepresentation of materials facts, and; to broaden the scope of certain permissive exclusion authorities. Finally, the proposed rule would revise current exclusion authorities in 42 CFR parts 1001, 1002, and 1005, to further clarify OIG's existing exclusion authorities. 4) Exceptions to the Beneficiary Inducement Prohibition for Certain Arrangements This proposed rule will codify section 6402(d)(2)(B) of the [ACA], entitled "Clarification of Treatment of Certain Charitable and Other Innocuous Programs."	

Appendix. (Continued)

Department/Agency	Title of Rule (RIN)	Abstract, as Provided in the Unified Agenda	Expected Publication Date
		Section 1128A(a)(5) of the [SSA] provides for a civil monetary penalty for certain inducements offered to Medicare and Medicaid beneficiaries. Section 6402(d)(2)(B) of the ACA adds four exceptions to the definition of remuneration at section 1128A(i)(6) of the [SSA] for purposes of section 1128A(a)(5): certain remuneration which promotes access to care and poses a low risk of harm to patients and Federal health care programs (as defined in section 1128(f) of the [SSA] and designated by the Secretary under regulations); certain offers or transfers in connection with retail rewards programs; certain unadvertised transfers of items or services to beneficiaries experiencing financial need; and certain waivers by PDP sponsors of Part D plans or MA organizations offering MA-PD plans of copayments otherwise owed by their enrollees for the first fill of a covered Part D drug that is a generic drug.	
DOL/EBSA	Ex Parte Cease and Desist and Summary Seizure Orders Under ERISA Section 521 (1210-AB48)	ERISA section 521, enacted under sec. 6605 of the Affordable Care Act (P.L. 111-148, 124 Stat. 780), authorizes the Secretary of Labor to issue a cease and desist order if it appears that a multiple employer welfare arrangement (MEWA) is fraudulent, creates an immediate danger to public safety or welfare, or can be reasonably expected to cause significant, imminent, and irreparable public injury. This section also authorizes the Secretary to issue a summary seizure order if it appears that a MEWA is in a financially hazardous condition. Regulatory guidance will provide standards for the issuance of such orders.	09/2011

Department/Agency	Title of Rule (RIN)	Abstract, as Provided in the Unified Agenda	Expected Publication Date
DOL/OWCP	Regulations Implementing Amendments to the Black Lung Benefits Act: Determining Coal Miners and Survivors Entitlement to Benefits (1240-AA04)	The Patient Protection and Affordable Care Act (PPACA) of 2010 amended the Black Lung Benefits Act, 30 U.S.C. 901 to 944, to reinstate two methods of establishing entitlement that were repealed with respect to claims filed after 1981. Specifically, the PPACA reinstated 30 U.S.C. 921(c)(4)(presumption of total disability or death due to pneumoconiosis arising out of coal mine employment where the miner had 15 years of coal mine employment and proof of total disability) and 30 U.S.C. 932(l) (automatic entitlement to benefits for eligible survivors of miners who were awarded benefits based on lifetime claims). The newly amended statutory provisions apply to claims filed after January 1, 2005, that are pending on or after PPACA's March 23, 2010 enactment date, and to all claims filed on or after March 23, 2010. The Department anticipates proposing rules that define the class of claims affected by the amendments and set the criteria for establishing entitlement to benefits under the amendments.	03/2012
TREAS/DO	Review and Approval Process for Waivers for State Innovation (1505-AC30)	This rule implements the procedures for developing, submitting and reviewing a Wavier for State Innovation described in section 1332 of the Patient Protection and the Affordable Care Act.	06/2011 Note: NPRM was published on 03/14/2011 (76 F.R. 13553).
TREAS/IRS	Branded Prescription Drug Fee (1545-BJ39)	Implementation of section 9008 applies to imposition of annual fee on branded prescription pharmaceutical manufacturers and importers, of the Patient Protection and Affordable Care Act of 2010, P.L. 111-148.	12/2011

Appendix. (Continued)

Department/Agency	Title of Rule (RIN)	Abstract, as Provided in the Unified Agenda	Expected Publication Date
TREAS/IRS	Development and Utilization of Uniform Explanation of Coverage Documents, Definitions, and Requirements To Provide Information Under the Patient Protection and Affordable Care Act (1545-BJ94)	These proposed regulations provide guidance concerning the development and utilization of uniform explanation of coverage documents, standardized definitions, and the provision of additional information under sections 2715 and 2715A of the Public Health Service Act, incorporated into section 9815 of the Internal Revenue Code by section 1563(f) of the Patient Protection and Affordable Care Act, P.L. 111-148.	06/2011 Note: No NPRM had been publishe as of 08/03/2011.
OPM	Federal Employees Group Life Insurance Program; Tribes and Tribal Organizations (3206-AM41)	The U.S. Office of Personnel Management (OPM) proposes to amend the Federal Employees Group Life Insurance regulations at 5 CFR chapter 87 to include enrollments for eligible employees of tribes and tribal organizations under the provisions of the Affordable Care Act of 2010.	12/2011
OPM OPM	Federal Employees Health Benefits Program; Tribes and Tribal Organizations (3206-AM40) Federal Employees Health Benefits Program; Disputed Claims and External Review Requirements (3206-AM42)	The U.S. Office of Personnel Management (OPM) proposes to amend the Federal Employees Health Benefits (FEHB) regulations at 5 CFR chapter 89 to include enrollments for eligible employees of tribes and tribal organizations under the provisions of the Affordable Care Act of 2010. The U.S. Office of Personnel Management (OPM) proposes to amend the Federal Employees Health Benefits (FEHB) regulations at 5 CFR chapter 89 to include changes to resolution of disputed health claims and to provide for external review under the provisions of the Affordable Care Act of 2010.	12/2011 12/2011

Department/Agency	Title of Rule (RIN)	Abstract, as Provided in the Unified Agenda	Expected Publication Date
Final Rules			
HHS/HRSA	Designation of Medically Underserved Populations and Health Professional Shortage Areas (0906-AA44)	This rulemaking is mandated under the Affordable Care Act. It requires the Secretary to establish a committee to draft an interim final rule for designation of Medically Underserved Populations (MUPs) and Primary Care Health Professions Shortage Areas (HPSAs). A notice of intent to form the negotiated rulemaking committee was published on May 21, 2010 (75 FR 26167) and the Secretary announced committee membership on July 21, 2010. The rulemaking committee consists of technical experts representing stakeholders that will be significantly affected by this rule. A variety of federal and state programs target resources to underserved populations using MUP and HPSA designations. These designations have not been updated in many cases for over 20 years and may not reflect current conditions in many areas. The task of the rulemaking committee is to update the designations, which will likely involve revisions to the current methodologies to reflect changes in the prevailing values of the indicators and availability of data on other indicators of underservice. Prior to passage of the Affordable Care Act, the Department made several attempts to revise the designations. An initial NPRM was published on September 1, 1998, but due to the extensive comments received, another notice was published on June 3, 1999 announcing a decision to develop and publish a revised NPRM for public comment. The second NPRM was published on February 29, 2008, with the comment period extended twice (first on April 21, 2008, and again on June 2, 2008). Substantial comments were received.	11/2011 Note: This rule is to be an interim final rule. Original NPRM was published 09/01/1998 (63 F.R. 46538). A second NRPM was published on 02/20/2008 and the comment period was extended twice.

Appendix. (Continued)

Department/Agency	Title of Rule (RIN)	Abstract, as Provided in the Unified Agenda	Expected Publication Date
		A Federal Register Notice published on July 23, 2008, announcing an Agency decision to carefully review these comments, develop a modified proposal, and publish another NPRM at a future date.	
HHS/CMS	Administrative Simplification: Adoption of Standard and Operating Rule for Electronic Funds Transfer (EFT) and Operating Rule for Remittance Advice (CMS-0024-IFC) (0938-AQ11)	This rule implements provisions of the Affordable Care Act of 2010 under Administrative Simplification that require the adoption of standards and operating rules for Electronic Funds Transfers (EFT) and operating rules for remittance advice, and to consider those operating rules developed by a qualified nonprofit entity that meets specific criteria.	12/2011 Note: Legal deadline for the final rule is 01/01/2012.
HHS/CMS	Administrative Simplification: Adoption of Authoring Organizations for Operating Rules and Adoption of Operating Rules for Eligibility and Claims Status (CMS-0032-IFC) (0938-AQ12)	This rule implements provisions of the Affordable Care Act of 2010 under Administrative Simplification that require the adoption of authoring organizations for operating rules and the adoption of operating rules for eligibility and claims status, and to consider those operating rules developed by a qualified nonprofit entity that meets specific criteria.	06/2011 Note: Legal deadline for the final rule was 07/01/2011. Rule was issued as an interim final rule on 07/08/2011 (76 F.R. 40458).
HHS/CMS	Medicaid Recovery Audit Contractors (CMS-6034-F) (0938-AQ19)	This final rule would provide guidance to States related to Federal/State funding of State start-up, operation and maintenance costs of Medicaid Recovery Audit Contractors (Medicaid RACs), and the payment methodology for State payments to Medicaid RACs in accordance with section 6411 of the Affordable Care Act.	08/2011 Note: NPRM was published on 11/10/2010 (75 F.R. 69037). Legal deadline for the final rule was 12/31/2010. No final rule was published as of 08/03/2011.

Department/Agency	Title of Rule (RIN)	Abstract, as Provided in the Unified Agenda	Expected Publication Date
		In addition, this rule includes requirements for States to assure that adequate appeals processes are in place for providers to dispute adverse determinations made by Medicaid RACs. Finally, the rule requires States and Medicaid RACs coordinate efforts with existing contractors and entities auditing Medicaid providers and with State and Federal law enforcement agencies.	
HHS/CMS	Payment Adjustment for Provider— Preventable Conditions Including Health Care-Acquired Conditions (CMS-2400-F) (0938-AQ34)	This rule, under the Affordable Care Act of 2010, would prohibit Medicaid payment for services related to health care acquired conditions.	06/2011 Note: NPRM was published on 02/17/2011 (76 F.R. 9283). Legal deadline for the final rule was 07/01/2011. Final rule was issued on 06/06/2011 (76 F.R. 32816).
HHS/CMS	Community First Choice Option (CMS-2337-F) (0938-AQ35)	This rule, under the Affordable Care Act of 2010, establishes an optional Medicaid benefit through which States could offer community-based attendant services and support to Medicaid beneficiaries with disabilities who would otherwise require the level of care offered in a hospital, nursing facility, or intermediate care facility for the mentally retarded.	08/2011 Note: NPRM was published on 02/25/2011 (76 F.R. 10736). No final rule was published as of 08/03/2011.
HHS/CMS	Changes to the Demonstration Review and Approval Process (CMS-2325-F) (0938-AQ46)	This rule implements provisions of the Affordable Care Act of 2010 and address concerns about transparency in the demonstration review and approval process. This rule establishes requirements for submitting new proposals and the requirements to amend or extend an approved demonstration project. This rule also provides guidance regarding public notice, monitoring, compliance, the evaluation of demonstration projects and the submission of reports to the Secretary for approved demonstrations.	07/2011 Note: NRPM was issued on 09/17/2010 (75 F.R. 56946). Legal deadline for the final rule was 09/19/2010. No final rule was published as of 08/03/2011.

Appendix. (Continued)

Department/Agency	Title of Rule (RIN)	Abstract, as Provided in the Unified Agenda	Expected Publication Date
HHS/CMS	Enhanced Federal Funding for Medicaid Eligibility Determination and Enrollment Activities (CMS-2346-F) (0938-AQ53)	The Affordable Care Act requires States' residents to apply, enroll, receive determinations, and participate in the State health subsidy programs known as "the Exchange". The Affordable Care Act requires many changes to State eligibility and enrollment systems and each State is responsible for developing a secure, electronic interface allowing the exchange of data. Existing legacy eligibility systems are not able to implement the numerous requirements. This rule is key to informing States about the higher rates that CMS will provide to help them update or build legacy eligibility systems that meet the ACA requirements.	06/2011 Note: NPRM was published on 11/08/2010 (75 F.R. 68583). Final rule was published on 04/19/2011 (76 F.R. 21950).
HHS/CMS	Internal Claims, Appeals, and External Review Processes Under the Affordable Care Act (CMS-9993-IFC2) (0938-AQ66)	The Affordable Care Act provides consumers with the right to appeal decisions made by their health carrier to an outside, independent decision maker, regardless on the State of residence or type of health insurance. Under interim final regulations issued earlier this year, non-grandfathered plans and issuers must comply with a State external review process or the Federal external review process. This rule would finalize the regulation and provide an opportunity to respond to public comments.	06/2011 Note: According to the Unified Agenda, the original interim final rule was issued on 07/23/2010 (75 F.R. 43330). A second interim final rule was published on 06/24/2011 (76 F.R. 37208), with technical corrections published on 07/26/2011 (76 F.R. 44491).
DOL/OSHA	Procedures for the Handling of Retaliation Complaints Under Section 1558 of the Affordable Care Act of 2010 (1218-AC55)	OSHA is promulgating procedures for the handling and investigation of retaliation complaints pursuant to section 1558 of the Patient Protection and Affordable Care Act of 2010 (the Affordable Care Act or ACA), which added section 18C to the Fair Labor Standards Act.	09/2011

Department/Agency	Title of Rule (RIN)	Abstract, as Provided in the Unified Agenda	Expected Publication Date
		This section established a new whistleblower protection statute to be administered by OSHA that provides protection from retaliation to employees who engage in protected activities under the ACA. Pursuant to the statute, the procedures will follow those enacted under the Consumer Product Safety Improvement Act, 15 U.S.C. 2087(b), including remedies and legal burdens of proof provisions. Promulgation of a regulation is necessary to govern whistleblower investigations conducted under the new statute.	
TREAS/IRS	Indoor Tanning Services (1545-BJ40)	Proposed regulations provide guidance on the indoor tanning services tax made by the Patient Protection and Affordable Care Act of 2010, affecting users and providers of indoor tanning services.	12/2011 Note: NPRM was published on 06/15/2010 (75 F.R. 33740).
TREAS/IRS	Development and Utilization of Uniform Explanation of Coverage Documents, Definitions, and Requirements To Provide Information Under the Patient Protection and Affordable Care Act (1545-BJ95)	These temporary regulations provide guidance concerning the development and utilization of uniform explanation of coverage documents, standardized definitions, and the provision of additional information under sections 2715 and 2715A of the Public Health Service Act, incorporated into section 9815 of the Internal Revenue Code by section 1563(f) of the Patient Protection and Affordable Care Act, P.L. 111-148.	06/2011 Note: No final rule was published as of 08/03/2011.
SSA	Regulations Regarding Income-Related Monthly Adjustment Amounts to Medicare Beneficiaries' Prescription Drug Premiums (3624F) (0960-AH22)	This subpart relates to section 1860D-13(a) of the Social Security Act (the Act), as added by section 3308 of the Patient Protection and Affordable Care Act (P.L. 111-111–148). Section 3308(a) establishes an income-related monthly adjustment (IRMAA) to the Medicare Part D premium.	08/2011 Note: Interim final rule was published on 12/07/2010 (75 F.R. 75884).

Appendix. (Continued)

Department/Agency	Title of Rule (RIN)	Abstract, as Provided in the Unified Agenda	Expected Publication Date
		Beneficiaries enrolled in Medicare Part D who have modified adjusted gross income over a threshold amount established in the statute will pay an IRMAA in addition to the Medicare Part D standard monthly premium and any applicable premium increases as described in 42 CFR 423.286. The regulations in this subpart explain how we decide whether you are required to pay an IRMAA, and if you are, the amount of your adjustment.	Legal deadline for the final rule was 12/31/2010. It appears that the agency will be issuing revisions to the interim final rule. As of 08/03/2011, no revisions had been published.

Source: Information in the first three columns is verbatim as reported in the Unified Agenda of Federal Regulatory and Deregulatory Actions, July 7, 2011, available at http://www.reginfo.gov/public/do/eAgendaMain. Information in the fourth column is from the Unified Agenda and the *Federal Register*. Note: The table includes only those Unified Agenda entries in which the Affordable Care Act was mentioned.

Although the CRA has been used only once to overturn an agency rule, Congress has regularly included provisions in the text of agencies' appropriations bills directing or preventing the development of particular regulations. Such provisions include prohibitions on the finalization of particular proposed rules, restrictions on certain types of regulatory activity, and restrictions on implementation or enforcement of certain provisions.[46] Appropriations provisions can also be used to prompt agencies to issue certain regulations, or to require that certain procedures be followed before or after their issuance. The inclusion of regulatory provisions in appropriations legislation as a matter of legislative strategy appears to arise from two factors: (1) Congress's ability via its "power of the purse" to control agency action, and (2) the fact that appropriations bills are considered "must pass" legislation. Congress's use of regulatory appropriations restrictions has fluctuated somewhat over time, and previous experience suggests such use they may be somewhat less frequent when Congress and the President are of the same party.[47]

End Notes

[1] For more information on PPACA, see CRS Report R40942, *Private Health Insurance Provisions in the Patient Protection and Affordable Care Act (PPACA)*, by Hinda Chaikind, Bernadette Fernandez, and Mark Newsom; CRS Report R41278, *Public Health, Workforce, Quality, and Related Provisions in PPACA: Summary and Timeline*, coordinated by C. Stephen Redhead and Erin D. Williams; CRS Report R41196, *Medicare Provisions in the Patient Protection and Affordable Care Act (PPACA): Summary and Timeline*, coordinated by Patricia A. Davis; and CRS Report R41210, *Medicaid and the State Children's Health Insurance Program (CHIP) Provisions in PPACA: Summary and Timeline*, by Evelyne P. Baumrucker et al.

[2] CRS Report R41180, *Rulemaking Requirements and Authorities in the Patient Protection and Affordable Care Act (PPACA)*, by Curtis W. Copeland.

[3] Henry J. Aaron and Robert D. Reischauer, "The War Isn't Over," *New England Journal of Medicine,* Health Care Reform Center, March 24, 2010, available at http://healthcarereform.nejm.org/?p=3223&query

[4] Although the law contains a number of deadlines for the issuance of rules, rulemaking deadlines are generally somewhat difficult to enforce, unless the statute itself contains an enforcement mechanism. None of the provisions in PPACA contain a legislative enforcement mechanism, so the remaining options for enforcement include political pressure on the agencies or civil litigation, although courts often defer to agencies' judgment on the timing of their issuance of a rule.

[5] CRS Report R41346, *Initial Final Rules Implementing the Patient Protection and Affordable Care Act*, by Curtis W. Copeland.

[6] Case law and guidance from OMB indicate that agencies should not attempt to bind affected parties through policy statements and other non-rule documents. See, for example, *Appalachian Power Co. v. Environmental Protection Agency*, 208 F.3d 1015 (D.C. Cir. 2000); and Office of Management and Budget, "Final Bulletin for Agency Good Guidance Practices," 72 *Federal Register* 3432, January 25, 2007, which states (on p. 3433) that "The courts, Congress, and other authorities have emphasized that rules which do not merely interpret existing law or announce tentative policy positions but which establish new policy positions that the agency treats as binding must comply with the (Administrative Procedure Act's) notice-and-comment requirements, regardless of how they initially are labeled."

[7] David H. Rosenbloom, *Building a Legislative-Centered Public Administration: Congress and the Administrative State, 1946-1999* (Tuscaloosa, AL: The University of Alabama Press, 2000), pp. 133-134.

[8] CRS Report R41180, *Rulemaking Requirements and Authorities in the Patient Protection and Affordable Care Act (PPACA)*, by Curtis W. Copeland.

[9] The current edition of the Unified Agenda is available at http://www.reginfo.gov/public/do/eAgendaMain.

[10] This requirement applies to all agencies covered by the Administrative Procedure Act (5 U.S.C. 551(1)).

[11] Executive Order 12866, "Regulatory Planning and Review," 58 *Federal Register* 51735, Oct. 4, 1993. Although most of the requirements in this executive order do not apply to independent regulatory agencies (e.g., the Securities and Exchange Commission), this section includes these agencies.

[12] RINs are assigned by RISC, and the Office of Management and Budget has asked agencies to include RINs in the headings of their rulemaking documents when they are published in the *Federal Register* to make it easer for the public and agency officials to track the publication history of regulatory actions. For a copy of this memorandum, see http://www.whitehouse.gov/sites/default/files/omb/assets

[13] Section 3(f) of Executive Order 12866 defines a "significant" regulatory action as one that is likely to result in a rule that may: "(1) Have an annual effect on the economy of $100 million or more or adversely affect in a material way the economy, a sector of the economy, productivity, competition, jobs, the environment, public health or safety, or State, local, or tribal governments or communities; (2) Create a serious inconsistency or otherwise interfere with an action taken or planned by another agency; (3) Materially alter the budgetary impact of entitlements, grants, user fees, or loan programs or the rights and obligations of recipients thereof; or (4) Raise novel legal or policy issues arising out of legal mandates, the President's priorities, or the principles set forth in this Executive order." Regulatory actions meeting the first of these four criteria are considered "economically significant." The definition of a "major" rule under the Congressional Review Act (5 U.S.C. §§801-808) is essentially the same as "economically significant."

[14] CRS Report R40713, *The Unified Agenda: Implications for Rulemaking Transparency and Participation*, by Curtis W. Copeland.

[15] PPACA was enacted on March 23, 2010. The first edition of the Unified Agenda following enactment of PPACA was issued on December 20, 2010. For a similar CRS report listing the rules pursuant to PPACA that were listed as upcoming in the December 20, 2010 edition of the Unified Agenda, see CRS Report R41586, *Upcoming Rules Pursuant to the Patient Protection and Affordable Care Act: Fall 2010 Unified Agenda*, by Curtis W. Copeland and Maeve P. Carey.

[16] Letter from Cass R. Sunstein, Administrator of the Office of Information and Regulatory Affairs, "Regulatory Policy Officers at Executive Departments and Agencies and Managing and Executive Directors of Certain Agencies and Commissions," January 21, 2011.

[17] E-mail from John C. Thomas, RISC Executive Director, August 3, 2011.

[18] In addition to the RINs, CMS included an agency-specific number as part of the title of the rule (e.g., CMS-1345-P). Those numbers are included as part of the title in the table in the Appendix.

[19] For a complete list of all the upcoming proposed rules listed in the Unified Agenda, their expected publication date, and information on when and if they were published, see the Appendix of this report.

[20] U.S. Department of Health and Human Services, Health Resources and Services Administration, "Exclusion of Orphan Drugs for Certain Covered Entities Under 340B Program," 76 *Federal Register* 29183, May 20, 2011.

[21] U.S. Department of Health and Human Services, Food and Drug Administration, "Food Labeling; Calorie Labeling of Articles of Food in Vending Machines," 76 *Federal Register* 19238, April 6, 2011.

[22] U.S. Department of Health and Human Services, Centers for Medicare & Medicaid Services, "Medicare Program; Availability of Medicare Data for Performance Measurement," 76 *Federal Register* 33566, June 8, 2011.

[23] U.S. Department of Health and Human Services, "Patient Protection and Affordable Care Act; Establishment of Consumer Operated and Oriented Plan (CO-OP) Program," 76 *Federal Register* 43237, July 20, 2011.

[24] U.S. Department of Health and Human Services, Food and Drug Administration, "Food Labeling; Calorie Labeling of Articles of Food in Vending Machines," 76 *Federal Register* 19238, April 6, 2011.

[25] U.S. Department of Health and Human Services, Food and Drug Administration, "Food Labeling; Nutrition Labeling of Standard Menu Items in Restaurants and Similar Retail Food Establishments," 76 *Federal Register* 19192, April 6, 2011.

[26] U.S. Department of Health and Human Services, Centers for Medicare & Medicaid Services, "Medicare Program; Medicare Shared Savings Program: Accountable Care Organizations," 76 *Federal Register* 68583, April 7, 2011.

[27] U.S. Department of Health and Human Services, "Patient Protection and Affordable Care Act; Establishment of Exchanges and Qualified Health Plans," 76 *Federal Register* 41866, July 15, 2011.

[28] Executive Order 12866 requires covered agencies (all except independent regulatory agencies like the Securities and Exchange Commission) to submit their "significant" rules to OIRA for review before publication as a proposed or final rule. For more information, see CRS Report RL32397, *Federal Rulemaking: The Role of the Office of Information and Regulatory Affairs*, by Curtis W. Copeland.

[29] U.S. Department of Health and Human Services, Centers for Medicare & Medicaid Services, "Medicaid Program; Face-to-Face Requirements for Home Health Services; Policy Changes and Clarifications Related to Home Health," 76 *Federal Register* 41032, July 12, 2011.

[30] For more information, see CRS Report RL34355, *The Regulatory Flexibility Act: Implementation Issues and Proposed Reforms*, by Curtis W. Copeland.

[31] U.S. Department of Health and Human Services, Centers for Medicare and Medicaid, "Administrative Simplification: Adoption of Operating Rules for Eligibility for a Health Plan and Health Care Claim Status Transactions," 75 *Federal Register* 40457, July 8, 2011.

[32] U.S. Department of Health and Human Services, Centers for Medicare and Medicaid, "Medicaid Program; Payment Adjustment for Provider-Preventable Conditions Including Health Care-Acquired Conditions," 76 *Federal Register* 32186, June 6, 2011.

[33] U.S. Department of Health and Human Services, Centers for Medicare and Medicaid, "Medicaid Program; Federal Funding for Medicaid Eligibility Determination and Enrollment Activities," 76 *Federal Register* 21950, April 19, 2011.

[34] This interim final rule was a joint rule. U.S. Department of the Treasury, Internal Revenue Service; U.S. Department of Labor, Employee Benefits Security Administration; and U.S. Department of Health and Human Services, Centers for Medicare and Medicaid, "Group Health Plans and Health Insurance Issuers: Rules Relating to Internal Claims and Appeals and External Review Processes," 76 *Federal Register* 37208, June 24, 2011.

[35] Interim final rules are a particular application of the "good cause" exception to notice-and comment rulemaking (5 U.S.C. § 553), in which the agency issues a final rule without a prior notice of proposed rulemaking, but with a post-promulgation opportunity for the public to comment. Interim final rules often take effect immediately, but the effective dates may also be delayed.

[36] The associated interim final rule was published on February 18, 2011 (76 *Federal Register* 9503).

[37] The associated interim final rule was published on June 28, 2010 (75 *Federal Register* 37188).

[38] The associated notice of proposed rulemaking was published on March 14, 2011 (76 F.R. 13553).

[39] The associated notice of proposed rulemaking was published on May 13, 2010 (75 F.R. 27141).

[40] For example, in *Sierra Club v. Costle* (657 F.2d 298, D.C. Cir. 1981), the D.C. Circuit concluded (at 409) that it was "entirely proper for congressional representatives vigorously to represent the interests of their constituents before administrative agencies engaged in informal, general policy rulemaking, so long as the individual Members of Congress do not frustrate the intent of Congress as a whole as expressed in statute, nor undermine applicable rules of procedure."

[41] Joint statement of House and Senate Sponsors, 142 *Cong. Rec.* E571, at E571 (daily ed. April 19, 1996); 142 *Cong. Rec.* S3683, at S3683 (daily ed. April 18, 1996).

[42] If a rule is considered "major" (e.g., has a $100 million annual effect on the economy), then the CRA generally prohibits it from taking effect until 60 days after the date that it is submitted to Congress.

[43] For a detailed discussion of CRA procedures, see CRS Report RL31160, *Disapproval of Regulations by Congress: Procedure Under the Congressional Review Act*, by Richard S. Beth.

[44] For more on the potential scope of the definition of a "rule" under the CRA, see CRS Report RL30116, *Congressional Review of Agency Rulemaking: An Update and Assessment of The Congressional Review Act after a Decade*, by Morton Rosenberg.

[45] The rule overturned in March 2001 was the Occupational Safety and Health Administration's ergonomics standard. This reversal was the result of a unique set of circumstances in which the incoming President (George W. Bush) did not veto the resolution disapproving the outgoing President's (William J. Clinton's) rule. See CRS Report RL30116, *Congressional Review of Agency Rulemaking: An Update and Assessment of The Congressional Review Act after a Decade*, by Morton Rosenberg, for a description of several possible factors affecting the CRA's use, and for other effects that the act may have on agency rulemaking.

[46] See CRS Report RL34354, *Congressional Influence on Rulemaking and Regulation Through Appropriations Restrictions*, by Curtis W. Copeland.

[47] Ibid., p. 35. This report indicated that some appropriations restrictions were repeated every year for 10 years, some were repeated several years in a row but then stopped, and some appeared in only one appropriations bill. Some restrictions appeared to be intended to stop particular rules issued at the end of presidential administrations.

In: Rules and Rulemaking in the Patient... ISBN: 978-1-61942-194-3
Editors: Raphael Kipp and Vince Caputo © 2012 Nova Science Publishers, Inc

Chapter 3

INITIAL FINAL RULES IMPLEMENTING THE PATIENT PROTECTION AND AFFORDABLE CARE ACT*

Curtis W. Copeland

SUMMARY

More than 40 provisions in the Patient Protection and Affordable Care Act (PPACA, P.L. 111-148, March 23, 2010, as amended) specifically require or permit federal agencies to issue regulations to implement the act's requirements. This report describes the final rules implementing PPACA that had been published in the *Federal Register* during the first 81/2 months of implementation.

As of December 7, 2010, at least 18 final rules had been issued implementing certain provisions in PPACA. An Appendix to this report lists these 18 final rules, including a summary of their requirements and their effective dates. PPACA specifically required that some of the rules be published. Other rules cited particular sections of PPACA as the statutory authority, but those sections did not specifically require the agencies to accomplish the underlying policy objectives through the rulemaking process. Most of the final rules were issued without a prior notice of proposed rulemaking, with the agencies often invoking the

* This is an edited, reformatted and augmented version of a Congressional Research Service publication, CRS Report for Congress R41346, from www.crs.gov, dated December 10, 2010.

"good cause" exception in the Administrative Procedure Act (APA, 5 U.S.C. §551 *et seq.)* for not allowing the public to comment before the final rules were issued. In several of the rules, the issuing agencies also stated that Congress had specifically authorized the issuance of final rules without first issuing a proposed rule. Most of the final rules permitted post-promulgation public comments, with the comment periods ending on or after the dates that the rules took effect. Most of the rules were considered "economically significant" (i.e., with an annual impact on the economy of at least $100 million), so the agencies provided estimates of their costs, benefits, and transfers.

INTRODUCTION

As discussed in a previous CRS report,[1] more than 40 provisions in the Patient Protection and Affordable Care Act (PPACA, P.L. 111-148, March 23, 2010, as amended) specifically require or permit federal agencies to issue regulations to implement the act's policy objectives. A number of these PPACA regulatory provisions require that the rules be issued or take effect by a certain date, and some of those deadlines occurred during the first several months of the act's implementation. For example:

- Section 10501(l) of the act requires the Secretary of the Department of Health and Human Services (HHS) to establish a grant program to (among other things) assist in the recruitment of students in underserved rural communities. The section also states "Not later than 60 days after the date of enactment of this section [i.e., by May 22, 2010], the Secretary shall by regulation define 'underserved rural community' for the purposes of this section."
- Section 1332(a)(4)(b) states that "the Secretary shall promulgate regulations relating to waivers under this section," and requires that the rule be promulgated within 180 days of enactment (i.e., by September 19, 2010).
- Section 10201(i) of PPACA states that the Secretary of the Department of Health and Human Services (HHS) "shall promulgate regulations relating to applications for, and renewals of, a demonstration project...," and requires that the rule be issued within 180 days of enactment (i.e., by September 19, 2010).

Federal agencies have begun issuing the regulations that were called for in PPACA. Also, agencies have issued other regulations citing the act's authority, even though PPACA does not specifically require or otherwise mention rulemaking in those areas.

This report describes the final rules that were published in the *Federal Register* within the first 81/2 months of the act's implementation (i.e., as of December 7, 2010).[2] An **Appendix** to this report lists these rules, including summaries of their requirements and their effective dates. The report will not be updated; its intent is to describe the initial rules being issued pursuant to PPACA, not to serve as an ongoing compendium of all PPACA-related rules.

FINAL RULES TO IMPLEMENT PPACA

As of December 7, 2010, federal agencies had issued at least 18 final rules implementing certain provisions in PPACA. The act specifically required that some of the rules be issued. For example:

- Section 6402(a) of PPACA required the Secretary of HHS to "promulgate a regulation that requires, not later than January 1, 2011, all providers of medical or other items or services and suppliers under the programs under titles XVIII and XIX that qualify for a national provider identifier to include their national provider identifier on all applications to enroll in such programs and on all claims for payment submitted under such programs." On May 5, 2010, the Centers for Medicare and Medicaid Services (CMS) within HHS published a final rule implementing this requirement.[3] The rule took effect on July 6, 2010.
- Section 1001 of PPACA added a new Section 2714 to the Public Health Service Act. Subsection (a) of the new section states that a "group health plan and a health insurance issuer offering group or individual health insurance coverage that provides dependent coverage of children shall continue to make such coverage available for an adult child (who is not married) until the child turns 26 years of age." Subsection (b) then states that "The Secretary shall promulgate regulations to define dependents to which coverage shall be made available under subsection (a)." On May 13, 2010, the Internal Revenue Service (IRS), the Employee Benefits Security Administration (EBSA) within the Department of Labor, and HHS

jointly published a final rule implementing this requirement.[4] The rule took effect on July 12, 2010, and it was generally applicable to group health plans, and to group and individual health insurance issuers, for plan years beginning on or after September 23, 2010.

- As noted previously in this report, Section 10501(l) of the act required the Secretary to issue a rule by May 22, 2010, defining the term "underserved rural community" for the purposes of a grant program designed to assist in the recruitment of students to those communities. On May 26, 2010, the Health Resources and Services Administration (HRSA) within HHS published a final rule pursuant to this directive.[5] The rule was effective on June 25, 2010.

Most Final Rules Not Specifically Required by PPACA

Other final rules cited particular sections of PPACA as the statutory authority, but those sections did not specifically require the agencies to accomplish the stated objectives through the rulemaking process. For example:

- On May 5, 2010, HHS published a final rule implementing the early retiree reinsurance program that was established by Section 1102 of PPACA.[6] Although that section of the act required the Secretary to establish this reinsurance program within 90 days after enactment (i.e., by June 21, 2010), it did not specifically state that the program had to be implemented through regulations. The rule took effect on June 1, 2010.
- Also on May 5, 2010, HHS published a final rule implementing a requirement in Section 1103(a) of PPACA (as amended by Section 10102(b) of the act) that the Secretary establish a mechanism, including an internet website, through with individuals in any state could identify affordable health insurance coverage options.[7] Although the act required the agency to develop a "standardized format" to be used in the presentation of this information, PPACA did not require that this mechanism and format be established through rulemaking. The rule took effect on May 10, 2010, and the website became active on July 1, 2010.
- On June 15, 2010, the IRS published a final rule providing guidance on the indoor tanning services excise tax imposed through Section 10907 of PPACA.[8] That section of the act requires that the tax be

remitted "at such time and in such manner as provided by the Secretary," but it does not specifically require the issuance of regulations.[9] The IRS rule took effect the day it was published, and applies to amounts paid after June 30, 2010. The rule expires on or before June 11, 2013.

- Section 1251 of PPACA states that certain provisions of the statute (subtitles A and C of Title I on "Immediate Improvements in Health Care Coverage for All Americans" and "Quality Health Insurance Coverage for All Americans," respectively) do not apply to group health plans and health insurance coverage in existence as of the date that the legislation was enacted (March 23, 2010). Although Section 1251 does not specifically require that new regulations be issued with regard to these "grandfathered" health plans, on June 17, 2010, the IRS, EBSA, and HHS jointly published a final rule implementing this section.[10] The rule became effective on June 14, 2010 (three days before it was published), although certain amendments took effect on July 12, 2010.
- On June 28, 2010, IRS, EBSA, and HHS jointly published a final rule implementing several new sections of the Public Health Service Act that were added by Section 1001 of PPACA: (1) Section 2704 (prohibiting preexisting condition exclusions); (2) Section 2711 (regarding lifetime and annual dollar limits on benefits); (3) Section 2712 (prohibiting rescissions); and (4) Section 2719A (regarding patient protections).[11] None of these four sections specifically required that new regulations be issued. The final rule takes effect on August 27, 2010, and is generally applicable to group health plans and group health issuers for plan years beginning on or after September 23, 2010. It is applicable to individual health insurance issuers for policy years beginning on or after January 1, 2014, except that for enrollees under the age of 19, the regulations apply for policy years starting on or after September 23, 2010.
- Section 1001 of PPACA also added a new Section 2713 to the Public Health Service Act on "Coverage of Preventive Health Services." On July 19, 2010, IRS, EBSA, and HHS published a final rule implementing this new section. Although PPACA required the Secretary of HHS to take certain actions (e.g., establishing when certain statutory provisions would take effect), the legislation did not specifically require that those actions be accomplished through the rulemaking process. The rule takes effect on September 17, 2010, and

applies to group health plans and insurers for plan years starting on or after September 23, 2010.

- In addition, Section 1001 of PPACA (and amendments in Section 10101) added a new Section 2719 to the Public Health Service Act regarding internal claims and appeals and external appeals processes for group health plans and health issuers that are not grandfathered plans. On July 23, 2010, IRS, EBSA, and HHS published a final rule implementing this new section.[12] Although PPACA allowed the Secretary of HHS to deem an existing external review process to be in compliance, it did not specifically require regulations. The rule takes effect on September 21, 2010, and applies to group health plans and insurers for plan years starting on or after September 23, 2010.

Although PPACA did not specifically require the agencies to issue any of these rules, the agencies' use of rulemaking to accomplish the underlying statutory objectives does not appear to be either improper or unusual. In fact, to the extent that those requirements were intended to be binding on the public, rulemaking may have been the agencies only viable option to implement the statutory provisions. For example, if an agency issues a guidance document, policy statement, or other non-rule document with the intent of legally binding the public, it could be subject to a possible judicial challenge for not having properly promulgated the policy through the APA rulemaking process. Case law and guidance from OMB indicate that agencies should not attempt to bind affected parties through policy statements and other non-rule documents.[13] Also, to the extent that PPACA changed existing regulatory requirements, new rules would have to be issued to amend those regulations.

No Prior Opportunity to Comment

The Administrative Procedure Act (APA, 5 U.S.C. §551 *et seq.*) establishes the basic requirements for the rulemaking process, and generally requires that federal agencies publish a notice of proposed rulemaking (NPRM) in the *Federal Register*, give "interested persons" an opportunity to comment on the proposed rule (usually at least 30 days), and after considering the public comments, publish a final rule. The APA also provides certain exceptions to the NPRM requirement. For example, 5 U.S.C. §553(b)(3)(B) permits agencies to issue final rules without a prior NPRM when the agency finds, for "good cause," that notice and comment procedures are "impracticable, unnecessary, or contrary to the public interest."[14] A process known as "interim final" rulemaking can be viewed as a particular application of the good cause exception, in which an agency issues a final rule without an NPRM, but with a post-promulgation opportunity for the public to comment. If the public comments persuade the agency that changes are needed in the interim final rule, the agency may revise the rule by publishing a final rule reflecting those changes.[15]

Most of the PPACA-related final rules that had been published as of December 7, 2010, were issued without pre-publication public comment. Twelve of the 18 final rules were issued as interim final rules. The issuing agencies frequently said that they invoked the APA's "good cause" exception to notice and comment because of the tight time constraints set by PPACA, and for other reasons. For example:

- In the May 5, 2010, rule on the early retiree insurance program, HHS noted that PPACA required the program to be established by June 21, 2010, but said that in a practical sense, the program had to begin operations by June 1, 2010. Because of the short time frame provided after the enactment of PPACA on March 23, 2010, HHS said "we find good cause to waive the notice of proposed rulemaking and to issue this final rule on an interim basis without prior comment."[16]
- In the May 26, 2010, rule on underserved rural communities, HHS stated that issuing a prior proposed rule and taking comments was "impractical" because the department was required to publish the rule within 60 days after the enactment of PPACA, and "those procedures take significantly longer than 60 days."[17] HHS also said that it believed it was unnecessary to undertake notice and comment because the rule would have limited impact, and because the funds for the program "might become available with little notice and awarding the funds quickly would serve an important public interest."[18]

In five final rules jointly issued by IRS, EBSA, and HHS,[19] the agencies indicated that Congress had specifically authorized the use of interim final rulemaking. All five of the rules contained the following language.

> Section 9833 of the Code, section 734 of ERISA (the Employee Retirement Income Security Act), and section 2792 of the (Public Health Service or PHS) Act authorize the Secretaries of the Treasury, Labor, and HHS (collectively, the Secretaries) to promulgate any interim final rules

> that they determine are appropriate to carry out the provisions of chapter 100 of the Code, part 7 of subtitle B of title I of ERISA, and part A of title XXVII of the PHS Act, which include PHS Act sections 2701 through 2728 and the incorporation of those sections into ERISA section 715 and Code section 9815.[20]

Even without specific statutory permission to issue these interim final rules, the agencies indicated that they would have done so under the "good cause" exception in Section 553(b) of the APA. For example, in the June 17 rule on "grandfathered health plans," the agencies said that even if the specific authorization for interim final rulemaking had not existed, "the Secretaries have determined that it would be impracticable and contrary to the public interest to delay putting the provisions in these interim final regulations in place until a full public notice and comment process was completed."[21] The agencies pointed out that numerous provisions of PPACA were applicable for plan years beginning on or after September 23, 2010 (six months after enactment), and that there was not sufficient time to draft and publish proposed rules, receive and consider comments, and draft and publish final regulations before that date.[22]

In most cases, the agencies issuing the rules provided explanations for why final rules were being issued without an NPRM. However, in the IRS rule on the indoor tanning services excise tax, the agency simply said that it had "been determined" that the notice and comment requirements of the Administrative Procedure Act did not apply to these regulations, but provided no further explanation (e.g., who made that determination, or why).[23]

All 12 of the interim final rules permitted the public a post-promulgation opportunity to comment. As *Table 1* below indicates, all of these rules took effect on or before the dates that the comment periods expired.

Costs, Benefits, and Transfers

Executive Order 12866 on "Regulatory Planning and Review" requires that covered agencies (generally, all executive branch agencies except independent regulatory agencies like the Securities and Exchange Commission) prepare a cost-benefit analysis before publishing any rule that the administrator of the Office of Information and Regulatory Affairs (OIRA) within the Office of Management and Budget (OMB) determines to be "economically significant."[24] The executive order defines a regulatory action as economically significant if it is expected to have at least a $100 million annual impact on the economy or "adversely affect in a material way the economy, productivity, competition, jobs, the environment, public health or safety, or State, local, or tribal government or communities." OMB Circular A-4 requires agencies to present the information in a standardized accounting statement, showing costs, benefits, and transfers separately.[25]

Table 1. Effective Dates and Comment Periods for PPACA Interim Final Rules

Publication Date	Agency/Agencies	Subject	Effective Date	End of Comment Period
05/05/10	HHS/CMS	National Provider Identifier	07/06/10	07/06/10
05/05/10	HHS	Web Portal Requirements	05/10/10	06/04/10
05/05/10	HHS	Early Retiree Insurance Program	06/01/10	06/04/10
05/13/10	IRS/EBSA/HHS	Coverage of Children to Age 26	07/12/10	08/11/10
05/26/10	HHS	Underserved Rural Communities	06/25/10	07/26/10
06/17/10	IRS/EBSA/HHS	Grandfathered Health Plans	06/14/10a	08/16/10
06/28/10	IRS/EBSA/HHS	Preexisting Condition Exclusions	08/27/10	08/27/10
07/19/10	IRS/EBSA/HHS	Preventive Services	09/17/10	09/17/10
07/23/10	IRS/EBSA/HHS	Internal Claims/ Appeals and External Review Processes	09/21/10	09/21/10
07/30/10	HHS/OCIIO	Pre-Existing Condition Insurance Plan Program	07/30/10	09/28/10
11/17/10	Treasury/IRS; DOL/EBSA; HHS/OCIIO	Amendment to Grandfathered Health Plans Rule	11/15/10	12/17/10
12/01/10	HHS/OCIIO	Medical Loss Ratio Requirements	01/01/11	01/31/11

Source: CRS, using information provided in the preambles to the agencies' rules. a. Certain amendments took effect July 12, 2010.

Table 2. Cost, Benefit, and Transfer Estimates of PPPACA Final Rules

Agency/Subject/Date	Annual Costs	Annual Benefits	Annual Transfers
HHS Early retiree reinsurance program 05/05/10	$39.8 million (paperwork costs).	HHS said the benefits were "not estimated."	$1,250 million (from the federal government to eligible sponsors and for the administration of the program).
IRS/EBSA/HHS Dependent coverage of children who have not attained age 26 05/13/10	$10.4 million (in 2010 dollars). Also, to the extent that the rule results in increased use of health care services, there will be additional costs to achieve the health benefits.	Qualitative benefits of expanding coverage options for the 19-25 population (mid-range estimate of 0.65 million), which should decrease the cost-shifting of uncompensated care onto those with insurance, increase preventive health care, and result in a healthier population. Also, greater job mobility.	$5,275 million (mid-range estimate; range from $3,483 million to $6,895 million). If premiums increase, there will be a transfer from individuals with family coverage who do not have dependents ages 19 to 25 from those who do have such dependents.
IRS/EBSA/HHS Grandfathered health plans 06/17/10	$24.7 million (mid-range estimate in 2010 dollars; range of $21.2 million to $26.9 million), due to the requirement to notify participants and beneficiaries, and to maintain documents.	Qualitative benefits of plan continuity; potentially slower rate of premium growth; incentives to employers to continue coverage; greater certainty about what changes can be made without affecting grandfather status.	Cost-sharing provisions may lead to transfers of wealth from premium payers overall to individuals using covered services. Subsequent changes could lead to transfers from non-grandfathered to grandfathered plans.
IRS/EBSA/HHS Preexisting condition exclusions, lifetime and annual dollar limits on benefits, rescissions, and patient protections 06/28/10	$4.9 million (in 2010 dollars).	Qualitative benefits of expanded coverage for children with preexisting conditions and individuals who face rescissions, lifetime limits, and annual limits as a result of high health costs. Also, improved health outcomes, improved worker productivity, and reduced financial strain.	Small transfer from those paying premiums in the group market to those obtaining the increased protections.

Agency/Subject/Date	Annual Costs	Annual Benefits	Annual Transfers
IRS/EBSA/HHS Coverage of preventive services under PPACA 07/19/10	Qualitative discussion of new costs to health care system when beneficiaries increase use of preventive services. Magnitude of increased use depends on "price elasticity of demand" and percentage change in prices facing those with reduced cost sharing or newly gaining coverage.	Qualitative benefits of expanding coverage and eliminating cost sharing, resulting in increased access and utilization of services, which are expected to result in reduced illnesses, reduced morbidity and mortality, increased productivity, and savings from lower health care costs.	Qualitative discussion of transfers expected to the extent that costs previously paid out-of-pocket now covered by group health plans and insurers. Risk pooling will result in higher average premiums. Rule expected to result in small transfer from those who use less preventive services to those who use more.
IRS/EBSA/HHS Internal claims and appeals and external review processes 07/23/10	$51.6 million	Qualitative benefits include a more uniform, rigorous, and consumer friendly system of claims and appeals processing, which will lead to a range of direct and indirect benefits (e.g., providing benefits consistent with the established terms of plans).	Reversals estimated at $24.4 million, part of which is a transfer from plans and issuers to those receiving payments for denied benefits.
HHS/OCIIO Pre-existing condition insurance plan program 07/30/10	$1,939,020 for reporting and recordkeeping	Qualitative benefits of increasing access to health care and reduced financial strain for participants. Also likely to improve health outcomes and worker productivity.	$5 billion in federal funds to contractors to aid in administering the program from 07/01/10 to 12/31/13.
HHS/CMS Hospital inpatient prospective payment systems for acute care hospitals 08/16/10	N/A	N/A	$440 million decrease in FY2011 operating payments and $21 million decrease in FY2011 capital payments. Long-term care hospitals expected to have an increase in payments of $22.5 million.

Table 2. (Continued)

Agency/Subject/Date	Annual Costs	Annual Benefits	Annual Transfers
HHS/CMS Updates the Home Health Prospective Payment System outlier policy 11/17/10	N/A	N/A	Net savings estimated at $960 million in calendar year 2011.
HHS/CMS Hospital outpatient prospective payment systems 11/24/10	N/A	N/A	Increased expenditures of about in FY2011 from OPPS provisions of $3.2 billion, and $230 million from ASC provisions.
HHS/CMS Payment policies under the physicians fee schedule 11/29/10	N/A	N/A	PPACA provisions estimated to increase expenditures by $1.97 billion.
HHS/OCIIO Medical loss ratio requirements 12/01/10	Mid-range estimated costs of $34.7 to $37.4 million per year in 2011 to 2013 for capturing and reporting data, and providing rebate notifications.	Qualitative benefits of increased transparency, increased quality of medical care, and improved health.	Mid-range estimated transfers of $863.5 million to $930 million in 2011 to 2013 from shareholders or stakeholders to enrollees.

Source: CRS, using information provided in the preambles to the agencies' rules.

Notes: Unless otherwise indicated, estimates are in 2010 dollars and reflect a 3% discount rate.

IRS did not indicate whether the June 15, 2010, rule on the indoor tanning services excise tax was economically significant or not, and did not provide any estimates of the rule's costs, benefits, or transfers. Several of the other final rules issued pursuant to PPACA were not considered economically significant, so the issuing agencies did not conduct a formal cost-benefit analysis or accounting statement. For example:

- In the May 5, 2010, rule on web portal requirements, HHS estimated that the total cost of the rule would be about $17 million in 2010, and about $15 million per year thereafter—well below the $100 million threshold to be considered economically significant.[26]
- CMS said that the May 5, 2010, rule requiring the use of National Provider Identification numbers was not economically significant because most providers and suppliers were already meeting the requirements.[27]
- HHS said that the May 26, 2010, rule on "underserved rural communities" was "technical in nature" and "will not change grant or funding eligibility for any other grant program."[28]
- CMS said that the November 15, 2010, rule on upper reimbursement limits withdrew those regulatory provisions that were superseded by PPACA, and was not economically significant.[29]
- OCIIO said that the November 17, 2010, rule amending the previously issued rule on "grandfathered" health plans was significant, but not economically significant.

However, other final rules issued pursuant to PPACA were considered economically significant by either OIRA or the issuing agencies because they were expected to have at least a $100 million impact on the economy. The issuing agencies provided information on their estimated costs, benefits, and transfers in the preambles to the rules. *Table 2* below summarizes that information.

CONCLUSION

Although Congress sometimes specifically requires or permits federal agencies to issue regulations on particular issues, the agencies can also decide to issue regulations to accomplish statutory requirements when not directed to do so. The initial regulations pursuant to PPACA are a clear illustration of that principle. The legislation contained more than 40 provisions that either required or permitted federal agencies to issue regulations, but most of the final rules issued pursuant to PPACA during the first 81/2 months after enactment were not specifically mentioned in the act. The agencies may be choosing to use rulemaking as opposed to other possible implementation mechanisms (e.g., guidance documents or policy memoranda) to carry out PPACA provisions because only regulations developed through the APA rulemaking process carry the force of law and can be binding on the public. If an agency attempts to bind the public through some mechanism other than a rule, the agency's actions could be subject to judicial review and possible reversal.

Similarly, although PPACA requires that certain final rules be issued without prior notice and comment,[30] federal agencies are also doing so without such requirements. The agencies frequently invoked the "good cause" exception to notice and comment provided in the APA, stating that the requirements in PPACA that certain programs be quickly implemented made it impractical for them to develop and publish a proposed rule, take comments on the proposal, and then develop and publish the final rule. The agencies also frequently said that it was similarly impractical for them to wait 30 days after publication to put those rules into effect (as is also generally required by the APA).

Although most of the PPACA-related final rules were issued without a prior opportunity for comment, the agencies did allow the public to comment on most of those rules after they were published. And even though the comment periods for these rules ended on or before the rules took effect, the agencies may still be persuaded to change them at some point in the future. Nevertheless, comments on final rules are generally believed to be less likely to result in changes to the rules than if comments were permitted prior to the final rules being published and made effective.[31] Because the agencies said that they were using interim final rulemaking because of tight deadlines in PPACA for rulemaking and implementation, as those deadlines become longer, it is possible that the agencies may be more willing to permit full notice and comment rulemaking.

Congressional Oversight Options

Congress has a range of tools available to oversee the rules that federal agencies are expected to issue to implement PPACA, including oversight hearings and confirmation hearings for the heads of regulatory agencies. Individual Members of Congress may also participate in the rulemaking process by, among other things, meeting with agency officials and filing public comments.[32] As one author indicated,

> [I]nvestigations conducted by congressional committees constitute another powerful device of formal political supervision.... The public legislative hearings, in which administrative action is carefully scrutinized and a commissioner or staff member is plied with questions, symbolizes the unparalleled sophistication of American congressional control over administrative action, in general and by [independent regulatory agencies], in particular. Individual oversight by representatives or senators also takes place. Through correspondence or meetings, the latter convey the concerns of their constituents.[33]

Another option is the Congressional Review Act (CRA, 5 U.S.C. §§801-808), which was enacted in 1996 in an attempt to reestablish a measure of congressional authority over rulemaking "without at the same time requiring Congress to become a super regulatory agency."[34] The act generally requires federal agencies to submit all of their covered final rules to both houses of Congress and GAO before they can take effect.[35] It also established expedited legislative procedures (primarily in the Senate) by which Congress may disapprove agencies' final rules by enacting a joint resolution of disapproval.[36] The definition of a covered rule in the CRA is quite broad, arguably including any type of document (e.g., legislative rules, policy statements, guidance, manuals, and memoranda) that the agency wishes to make binding on the affected public.[37] After these rules are submitted, Congress can use the expedited procedures specified in the CRA (particularly in the Senate) to disapprove any of the rules. CRA resolutions of disapproval must be presented to the President for signature or veto.

For a variety of reasons, however, the CRA has been used to disapprove only one rule in the 14 years since it was enacted.[38] Perhaps most notably, it is likely that a President would veto a resolution of disapproval to protect rules developed under his own administration, and it may be difficult for Congress to muster the two-thirds vote in both houses needed to overturn the veto. Congress can also use regular (i.e., non-CRA) legislative procedures to disapprove agencies' rules, but such legislation may prove even more difficult to enact than a CRA resolution of disapproval (primarily because of the lack of expedited procedures in the Senate), and if enacted may also be vetoed by the President.

Appendix. Final Rules Implementing PPACA (as of December 7, 2010)

Publication Date/Citation	Department/Agency or Office	Summary	Dates
May 5, 2010 75 Federal Register 24437	Department of Health and Human Services (HHS)/Centers for Medicare and Medicaid Services (CMS)	Interim final rule implementing the requirement in Section 6402(a) of PPACA that providers of medical or other items or services to include their National Provider Identifier (NPI) on all applications to enroll and on all claims for payment. The rule also requires physicians and eligible professionals to order and refer covered items to be enrolled in Medicare, and adds requirement to provide documentation on referrals to programs at high risk of waste and abuse.	Effective on July 6, 2010. Comment period ended July 7, 2010.
May 5, 2010 75 Federal Register 24470	HHS/Office of the Secretary	Interim final rule implementing the requirement in Section 1103(a) of PPACA to establish a website through which individuals and small businesses can obtain information about the insurance coverage options available in their state. The rule adopts the categories of information that will be collected and displayed, and the data required from issuers and requested from states, associations, and high risk pools.	Effective on May 10, 2010. The initial version of the website became available July 1, 2010. Comment period ended June 4, 2010.

Appendix. (Continued)

Publication Date/Citation	Department/Agency or Office	Summary	Dates
May 5, 2010 75 Federal Register 24450	HHS/Office of the Secretary	Interim final rule implementing the Early Retiree Reinsurance Program in Section 1102 of PPACA. This temporary program (ends by January 1, 2014) provides reimbursement to participating employment-based plans for a portion of the cost of health benefits for early retirees and their spouses/dependents (certain claims between $15,000 and $90,000).	Effective on June 1, 2010. Comment period ended June 4, 2010.
May 13, 2010 75 Federal Register 27122	Department of the Treasury(Treasury)/Internal Revenue Service (IRS); Department of Labor (DOL)/Employee Benefits Security Administration (EBSA); HHS	Interim final rule implementing the requirements in Section 1001 of PPACA for group health plans and health insurance coverage in the group and individual markets regarding dependent coverage of children who have not attained age 26.	Effective on July 12, 2010. The requirements generally apply for plan years beginning on or after September 23, 2010. Comment period ended August 11, 2010.
May 26, 2010 75 Federal Register 29447	HHS	Interim final rule (required by Section 10501(l) of PPACA) defining "underserved rural community" for purposes of the Rural Physician Training Grant Program in Section 749B of the Public Health Service Act.	Effective on June 25, 2010. Comment period ended July 26, 2010.

Publication Date/Citation	Department/Agency or Office	Summary	Dates
June 15, 2010 75 Federal Register 33683	Treasury/IRS	Final and temporary rules providing guidance on the indoor tanning services excise tax imposed by Section 10907 of PPACA.	Effective on June 15, 2010 The tax applies to payments after June 30, 2010. No comments requested.
June 17, 2010 75 Federal Register 34538	Treasury/IRS; DOL/EBSA; HHS	Interim final rule implementing the rules for group health plans and health insurance coverage in the group and individual markets regarding status as a "grandfathered" health plan (Section 1251 of PPACA).	Effective on June 14, 2010, except that certain amendments are effective July 12, 2010. Comment period ended August 10, 2010.
June 28, 2010 75 Federal Register 37188	Treasury/IRS; DOL/EBSA; HHS	Interim final rule implementing the rules for group health plans and health insurance coverage in the group and individual markets regarding preexisting condition exclusions, lifetime and annual dollar limits on benefits, rescissions, and patient protections (Sections 2704, 2711, 2712, and 2719A of PPACA).	Effective on August 27, 2010. Some of the requirements apply for plan years starting on or after September 23, 2010, while other requirements begin for plan years starting on or after January 1, 2014. Comment period ended August 27, 2010.
July 19, 2010 75 Federal Register 41726	Treasury/IRS; DOL/EBSA; HHS	Interim final rule implementing the requirements for group health plans and health insurance coverage in the group and individual markets (Section 2713 of the Public Health Service Act as revised by PPACA).	Effective on September 17, 2010. Applicable to group health plans and group health insurers for plan years beginning on or after September 23, 2010. Comment period ended September 17, 2010.

Appendix. (Continued)

Publication Date/Citation	Department/Agency or Office	Summary	Dates
July 23, 2010 75 Federal Register 43330	Treasury/IRS; DOL/EBSA; HHS	Interim final rule implementing the requirements regarding internal claims and appeals and external review processes for group health plans and health insurance coverage in the group and individual markets (Section 2719 of the Public Health Service Act as revised by PPACA).	Effective September 21, 2010. Applicable to group health plans and group health insurers for plan years beginning on or after September 23, 2010. Comment period ended September 21, 2010.
July 30, 2010 75 Federal Register 45014	HHS/Office of Consumer Information and Insurance Oversight (OCIIO)	Interim final rule implementing the requirement in Section 1101 of PPACA regarding the establishment of a temporary high risk insurance pool program to provide coverage to uninsured individuals with pre-existing conditions.	Effective on July 30, 2010. Comment period ended September 28, 2010.
August 16, 2010 75 Federal Register 50042	HHS/CMS	Final rule revising the Medicare hospital inpatient prospective payment systems for operating and capital-related costs of acute care hospitals to (among other things) implement certain provisions in PPACA.	Effective on October 1, 2010. (Proposed rule was published May 4, 2010.)
November 15, 2010 75 Federal Register 69591	HHS/CMS	Final rule implementing Section 2503(a) of PPACA by withdrawing provisions on upper reimbursement limits and other matters.	Effective on December 15, 2010. (Proposed rule was published September 3, 2010.)

Publication Date/Citation	Department/Agency or Office	Summary	Dates
November 17, 2010 75 Federal Register 70114	Treasury/IRS; DOL/EBSA; HHS/OCIIO	Interim final rule amending the June 17, 2010, interim final rule on “grand-fathered” health plans. The amendment permits certain changes in policies, certificates, or contracts of insurance without loss of “grandfathered” status.	Effective on November 15, 2010. Comment period ended December 17, 2010.
November 17, 2010 75 Federal Register 70372	HHS/CMS	Final rule that (among other things) updates the Home Health Prospective Payment System outlier policy in accordance with Section 3131 of PPACA.	Effective on January 1, 2011. (Proposed rule was published July 23, 2010.)
November 24, 2010 75 Federal Register 71800	HHS/CMS	Final rule implementing PPACA provisions regarding (1) the Medicare hospital outpatient prospective payment system, (2) the Medicare ambulatory surgical center payment system, (3) payments to hospitals for direct graduate medical education and indirect medical education costs, and (4) limitations on certain physician referrals to hospitals in which they have a financial interest.	Effective on January 1, 2011, except certain provisions effective on December 2, 2010. Various applicability dates. Comment period ends January 3, 2011.
November 29, 2010 75 Federal Register 73170	HHS/CMS	Final rule with comment period addressing changes to the physician fee schedule and other Medicare Part B policies. Among other things, the rule “addresses, implements, or discusses” provisions in PPACA.	Effective on January 1, 2011. Comment period ends January 3, 2011.

Appendix. (Continued)

Publication Date/Citation	Department/Agency or Office	Summary	Dates
December 1, 2010 75 Federal Register 74864	HHS/OCIIO	Interim final rule implementing medical loss ratio requirements for health insurers under Section 2718(a)-(c) of the Public Health Service Act as amended by PPACA.	Effective on January 1, 2011. Comment period ends January 31, 2011.

Source: CRS, using information provided in the preambles to the agencies' rules.

Although the CRA has been used only once to overturn an agency rule, Congress has regularly included provisions in the text of agencies' appropriations bills directing or preventing the development of particular regulations. Such provisions include prohibitions on the finalization of particular proposed rules, restrictions on certain types of regulatory activity, and restrictions on implementation or enforcement of certain provisions.[39] Appropriations provisions can also be used to prompt agencies to issue certain regulations, or to require that certain procedures be followed before or after their issuance. The inclusion of regulatory provisions in appropriations legislation as a matter of legislative strategy appears to be prompted by two factors: (1) Congress's ability via its "power of the purse" to control agency action, and (2) the fact that appropriations bills are considered "must pass" legislation. Congress's use of regulatory appropriations restrictions has fluctuated somewhat over time, and previous experience suggests that they may be somewhat less frequent when Congress and the President are of the same party.[40]

End Notes

[1] See CRS Report R41180, Regulations Pursuant to the Patient Protection and Affordable Care Act (PPACA), by Curtis W. Copeland, for a summary of the provisions that required or permitted rulemaking. Shortly after PPACA was enacted, Congress passed and the President signed the Health Care and Education Reconciliation Act of 2010 (HCERA, P.L. 111-152, March 30, 2010), which amended various health care and revenue provisions in PPACA. This report considers both acts under the general heading of PPACA.

[2] To identify these rules and documents, CRS conducted searches through the electronic Federal Register at GPO Access (http://www.gpoaccess.gov/fr/advanced.html) using the term "Patient Protection and Affordable Care Act." Rules in which PPACA was mentioned but not cited as the statutory authority were eliminated from the search results.

[3] U.S. Department of Health and Human Services, Centers for Medicare and Medicaid Services, "Medicare and Medicaid Programs; Changes in Provider and Supplier Enrollment, Ordering and Referring, and Documentation Requirements; and Changes in Provider Agreements," 75 Federal Register 24437, May 5, 2010.

[4] U.S. Department of the Treasury, Internal Revenue Service; Department of Labor, Employee Benefits Security Administration; Department of Health and Human Services, "Group Health Plans and Health Insurance Issuers Relating to Dependent Coverage of Children to Age 26 Under the Patient Protection and Affordable Care Act; Interim Final Rule and Proposed Rule," 75 Federal Register 27122, May 13, 2010.

[5] U.S. Department of Health and Human Services, Health Resources and Services Administration, "Publish Health Service Act, Rural Physician Training Grant Program, Definition of 'Underserved Rural Community,'" 75 Federal Register 29447, May 26, 2010.

[6] U.S. Department of Health and Human Services, Office of the Secretary, "Early Retiree Reinsurance Program," 75 Federal Register 24450, May 5, 2010. This program provides reimbursement to participating employment-based plans for a portion of the cost of health benefits for early retirees and their spouses, surviving spouses, and dependents.

[7] U.S. Department of Health and Human Services, Office of the Secretary, "Health Care Reform Insurance Web Portal Requirements," 75 Federal Register 24470, May 5, 2010. The address of this website is http://www.healthcare.gov/.

[8] U.S. Department of the Treasury, Internal Revenue Service, "Indoor Tanning Services; Cosmetic Services; Excise Taxes," 75 Federal Register 33683, June 15, 2010.

[9] It does, however, state that every person receiving a payment for services on which a tax is imposed "shall collect the amount of the tax from the individual on whom the service is performed and remit such tax quarterly to the Secretary at such time and in such manner as provided by the Secretary."

[10] U.S. Department of the Treasury, Internal Revenue Service; Department of Labor, Employee Benefits Security Administration; Department of Health and Human Services, "Group Health Plans and Health Insurance Coverage Relating to Status as a Grandfathered Health Plan Under the Patient Protection and Affordable Care Act; Interim Final Rule and Proposed Rule," 75 Federal Register 34538, June 17, 2010.

[11] U.S. Department of the Treasury, Internal Revenue Service; Department of Labor, Employee Benefits Security Administration; Department of Health and Human Services, "Patient Protection and Affordable Care Act: Preexisting Condition Exclusions, Lifetime and Annual Limits, Rescissions, and Patient Protections," 75 Federal Register 37188, June 28, 2010.

[12] U.S. Department of the Treasury, Internal Revenue Service; Department of Labor, Employee Benefits Security Administration; Department of Health and Human Services, "Interim Final Rules for Group Health Plans and Health Insurance Issuers Relating to Internal Claims and Appeals and External Review Processes Under the Patient Protection and Affordable Care Act," 75 Federal Register 43330, July 23, 2010.

[13] See, for example, Appalachian Power Co. v. Environmental Protection Agency, 208 F.3d 1015 (D.C. Cir. 2000); and Office of Management and Budget, "Final Bulletin for Agency Good Guidance Practices," 72 Federal Register 3432, January 25, 2007, which states (on p. 3433) that "The courts, Congress, and other authorities have emphasized that rules which do not merely interpret existing law or announce tentative policy positions but which establish new policy positions that the agency treats as binding must comply with the (Administrative Procedure Act's) notice-and-comment requirements, regardless of how they initially are labeled."

[14] 5 U.S.C. §553(b).

[15] For more information, see Michael Asimow, "Interim Final Rulemaking: Making Haste Slowly," Administrative Law Review, 51 (Summer 1999), pp. 703-755.

[16] 75 Federal Register 24460.

[17] 75 Federal Register 29448.

[18] Ibid.

[19] These were the May 13 rule on dependent coverage of children to age 26; the June 17 rule on "grandfathered" health plans; the June 28 rule on preexisting condition exclusions and other matters; the July 19 rule on preventive services; and the July 23 rule on internal claims and appeals and external review processes.

[20] See, for example, 75 Federal Register 2715; 75 Federal Register 34545; 75 Federal Register 37195; and 75 Federal Register 41729.

[21] 75 Federal Register 34545.

[22] Agencies often publish final rules without prior proposed rules, and frequently cite the "good cause" exception. For example, in 1998, GAO determined that about half of the 4,000 final rules published that year had no prior NPRM, and that the agencies most commonly cited the "good cause" exception. See U.S. General Accounting Office, Federal Rulemaking: Agencies Often Published Final Actions Without Proposed Rules, GAO-98-126, August 31, 1998.

[23] 75 Federal Register33685. IRS also said that it had "been determined" that the rule was not a "significant regulatory action" as defined in Executive Order 12866, so a regulatory assessment was not required. The rule was not reviewed by the Office of Information and Regulatory Affairs at the Office of Management and Budget prior to publication.

[24] The President, Executive Order 12866, "Regulatory Planning and Review," 58 Federal Register 51735. The cost-benefit requirements are in Section 6(a)(3)(C) of the order. The definition of an "economically significant" rule is in Section 3(f)(1) of the order.

[25] See http://www.whitehouse.gov/omb/circulars/a004/a-4.pdf for a copy of OMB Circular A-4. Transfers occur when wealth or income is redistributed without any direct change in aggregate social welfare (e.g., federal Medicare payments to doctors and hospitals).

[26] 75 Federal Register 24480.

[27] 75 Federal Register 24447.

[28] 75 Federal Register 29450.

[29] 75 Federal Register 69596.

[30] For example, Section 1104(b)(2) of PPACA requires that the Secretary of HHS promulgate two interim final rules.

[31] For example, although the Administrative Conference of the United States endorsed the use of interim final and direct final rulemaking, it also said that "prepromulgation comment is generally considered preferable because agencies are perceived by commenters as more likely to accept changes in a rule that has not been promulgated as a final rule— and potential commenters are more likely to file comments in advance of the agency's 'final' determination." See "Recommendation 95-4, Procedures for Noncontroversial and Expedited Rulemaking," available at http://www.law.fsu.edu/library/admin/acus/305954.html.

[32] In Sierra Club v. Costle (657 F.2d 298, D.C. Cir. 1981), the D.C. Circuit concluded (at 409) that it was "entirely proper for congressional representatives vigorously to represent the interests of their constituents before administrative agencies engaged in informal, general policy rulemaking, so long as the individual Members of Congress do not frustrate the intent of Congress as a whole as expressed in statute, nor undermine applicable rules of procedure."

[33] Dominique Custos, "The Rulemaking Power of Independent Regulatory Agencies," The American Journal of Comparative Law, vol. 54 (Fall 2006), p. 633.

[34] Joint statement of House and Senate Sponsors, 142 Cong. Rec. E571, at E571 (daily ed. April 19, 1996); 142 Cong. Rec. S3683, at S3683 (daily ed. April 18, 1996).

[35] If a rule is considered "major" (e.g., has a $100 million annual effect on the economy), then the CRA generally prohibits it from taking effect until 60 days after the date that it is submitted to Congress.

[36] For a detailed discussion of CRA procedures, see CRS Report RL31160, Disapproval of Regulations by Congress: Procedure Under the Congressional Review Act, by Richard S. Beth.

[37] For more on the potential scope of the definition of a "rule" under the CRA, see CRS Report RL30116, Congressional Review of Agency Rulemaking: An Update and Assessment of The Congressional Review Act after a Decade, by Morton Rosenberg.

[38] The rule overturned in March 2001 was the Occupational Safety and Health Administration's ergonomics standard. This reversal was the result of a unique set of circumstances in which the incoming President (George W. Bush) did not veto the resolution disapproving the outgoing President's (William J. Clinton's) rule. See CRS Report RL30116, Congressional Review of Agency Rulemaking: An Update and Assessment of The Congressional Review Act after a Decade, by Morton Rosenberg, for a description of several possible factors affecting the CRA's use, and for other effects that the act may have on agency rulemaking.

[39] See CRS Report RL34354, Congressional Influence on Rulemaking and Regulation Through Appropriations Restrictions, by Curtis W. Copeland.

[40] Ibid., p. 35. This report indicated that some appropriations restrictions were repeated every year for 10 years, some were repeated several years in a row but then stopped, and some appeared in only one appropriations bill. Some restrictions appeared to be intended to stop particular rules issued at the end of presidential administrations.

INDEX

A

abuse, 93
access, 9, 64, 87
accounting, 85, 89
accreditation, 54
adjustment, 71, 72
age, 5, 20, 61, 79, 81, 86, 94, 100
appointments, 3, 35
appropriations, 2, 24, 32, 49, 76, 92, 101
assessment, 53, 100
assets, 74
audit, 69
authorities, 63, 73, 100
authority, vii, 1, 2, 3, 4, 21, 22, 23, 33, 34, 35, 36, 48, 62, 63, 79, 91

B

banks, 50
beneficiaries, 8, 9, 11, 61, 62, 63, 64, 69, 86, 87
benefits, viii, 7, 11, 12, 17, 18, 19, 22, 31, 60, 65, 78, 81, 85, 86, 87, 88, 89, 94, 95, 99
bonds, 54
businesses, 31, 42, 59

C

caloric intake, 9, 27
caregivers, 8
certification, 7, 26, 56
children, 5, 9, 79, 86, 94, 100
citizens, 54
clarity, 51
classes, 11
clinical trials, 62
coal, 65
collisions, 31
communities, 14, 74, 78, 80, 83, 85, 89
community, 8, 14, 27, 53, 61, 69, 78, 80, 94
community-based services, 53
competition, 74, 85
compliance, 8, 57, 60, 69, 82
consensus, 12, 22
constituents, 23, 31, 75, 91, 101
consumers, 18, 59, 70
controversies, 21
coordination, 8, 58
cost, 17, 20, 22, 31, 59, 62, 84, 86, 87, 89, 94, 99, 100
cost-benefit analysis, 84, 89

D

danger, 64
deaths, 31
delegates, vii, 2, 33, 34, 35
demonstrations, 69
denial, 17
disability, 61, 65
disclosure, 8, 9, 50, 59, 60

discrimination, 17, 61
doctors, 100
draft, 67, 84
drugs, 11, 51, 56, 62

E

education, 97
emergency, 19, 62
employees, 19, 66, 71
employers, 86
employment, 65, 94, 99
enforcement, 18, 24, 49, 73, 92
enrollment, 6, 7, 19, 20, 26, 54, 57, 58, 61, 70
environment, 74, 85
equipment, 55
ergonomics, 32, 76, 101
exclusion, 17, 63
expenditures, 88
expertise, 3
extracts, 55

F

families, 34
financial, 51, 61, 64, 86, 87, 97
financial incentives, 51
flexibility, 42, 45
fluid, 37
force, 3, 36, 90
fraud, 20, 57, 58
funding, 68, 89
funds, 13, 25, 60, 83

G

governments, 42, 45, 74
grants, 2, 7, 13, 21, 26, 59, 74
growth, 34, 86
guidance, 2, 5, 15, 16, 17, 22, 23, 28, 35, 48, 54, 56, 64, 66, 68, 69, 71, 73, 80, 82, 90, 91, 95
guidelines, 15

H

harbors, 61
hiring, 19
history, 74
hospice, 15, 27
hospitalization, 5
host, 15
housing, 20
human, 9

I

images, 31
imagination, 3, 35
income, 7, 71, 72, 100
increased access, 87
individuals, 7, 11, 34, 53, 54, 58, 59, 80, 86, 93, 96
ingredients, 9
injuries, 31
integrity, 57
interface, 70
investment, 7, 27
issues, 2, 22, 30, 36, 75, 82, 83, 89

J

job mobility, 86

L

labeling, 18, 51, 52
law enforcement, 69
laws, 13
lead, 86, 87
legislation, vii, 1, 2, 3, 4, 5, 21, 24, 30, 33, 34, 35, 36, 48, 49, 81, 90, 91, 92
legislative authority, 3, 47
lifetime, 65, 81, 86, 95
light, 53
litigation, 12, 15, 73
loans, 13, 26, 60

long-term services, 8
low risk, 64

M

manufacturing, 51
marketing, 7
marketplace, 51
materials, 63
membership, 67
methodology, 6, 11, 15, 26, 27, 50, 68
misuse, 63
morbidity, 87
mortality, 87

N

national origin, 61
negotiation, 15
nursing, 5, 69
nutrient, 9, 27
nutrition, 51, 52

O

officials, 2, 3, 23, 35, 48, 74, 91
operations, 83
opportunities, 4
outpatient, 5, 51, 56, 88, 97
oversight, 2, 4, 23, 34, 36, 48, 53, 57, 90, 91

P

participants, 86, 87
penalties, 6, 25, 62, 63
permit, vii, viii, 1, 2, 4, 15, 19, 22, 33, 34, 35, 36, 63, 77, 78, 90
pharmaceutical, 65
physicians, 88, 93
platinum, 19
pneumoconiosis, 65
policy, viii, 2, 4, 5, 15, 19, 23, 31, 48, 50, 56, 73, 74, 76, 77, 78, 81, 82, 88, 90, 91, 97, 100, 101
policy issues, 74
pools, 93
population, 19, 86
prescription drugs, 18, 19, 56
price elasticity, 87
principles, 74
private sector, 22
professionals, 93
profit, 7, 10, 28, 42
project, 7, 14, 27, 69, 78
proposed regulations, 14, 18, 27, 29, 66
protection, 71
publishing, 30, 83, 84

Q

quality assurance, 53
query, 30, 31, 73

R

race, 61
recognition, 16, 28
recommendations, 10, 13
reconciliation, 4, 30
rehabilitation, 5
reinsurance, 80, 86
requirements, vii, viii, 1, 2, 4, 5, 7, 8, 9, 10, 12, 13, 14, 19, 20, 21, 22, 26, 29, 30, 31, 34, 35, 36, 37, 42, 45, 47, 50, 51, 52, 54, 55, 59, 69, 70, 73, 77, 79, 82, 84, 88, 89, 90, 94, 95, 96, 98, 100
resolution, 23, 32, 37, 48, 66, 76, 91, 101
resources, 8, 61, 67
response, 46
restaurants, 9, 52
restrictions, 2, 16, 24, 32, 49, 76, 92, 101
retail, 9, 52, 64
retaliation, 70, 71
revenue, 4, 6, 99
rewards, 64

rights, 74
rules, vii, viii, 2, 3, 4, 5, 10, 13, 15, 17, 19, 20, 21, 22, 23, 24, 25, 26, 28, 29, 31, 32, 33, 34, 35, 36, 37, 38, 39, 40, 41, 42, 43, 44, 45, 46, 47, 48, 49, 60, 61, 65, 68, 73, 74, 75, 76, 77, 78, 79, 80, 82, 83, 84, 85, 88, 89, 90, 91, 92, 95, 98, 99, 100, 101

S

safety, 50, 74, 85
sanctions, 50
savings, 16, 22, 28, 51, 55, 87, 88
savings account, 16, 22, 28
scope, 32, 63, 76, 101
seizure, 64
services, 5, 8, 9, 15, 18, 19, 27, 53, 55, 61, 62, 64, 69, 71, 79, 80, 84, 86, 87, 89, 93, 95, 99, 100
sex, 61
shareholders, 88
shortage, 11, 27
showing, viii, 34, 37, 85
silver, 19
small businesses, 42, 45, 59, 93
stakeholder groups, 18
stakeholders, 67, 88
standardization, 9
statutes, vii, 1, 2, 9, 21, 22, 31, 34, 47
statutory authority, viii, 77, 80, 99
statutory provisions, 35, 65, 81, 82
structure, 13, 25
subpoena, 63
subsidy, 70
supervision, 23, 91
supplier, 54, 57, 62
suppliers, 55, 57, 58, 62, 79, 89
survivors, 65

T

target, 12, 67
taxes, 7, 28
techniques, 5
technology, 31
time constraints, 14, 83
time frame, 12, 83
training, 9
transactions, 55
transparency, 36, 69, 88
transportation, 62
tribal officials, 37

U

uniform, viii, 33, 37, 66, 71, 87
uninsured, 31, 96
updating, 10
urban, 53

V

variations, 9
varieties, 9
veto, 23, 32, 48, 76, 91, 101
vote, 23, 48, 91

W

waiver, 8, 13, 53, 63
war, 3, 35
waste, 93
wealth, 86, 100
web, 89
welfare, 64
workers, 9
workload, 3

Y

yield, 22